Day-to-Day Assessment in the Reading Workshop

Making Informed Instructional Decisions in Grades 3–6

Franki Sibberson
and Karen Szymusiak

SCHOLASTIC

NEW YORK ◆ TORONTO ◆ LONDON ◆ AUCKLAND ◆ SYDNEY
MEXICO CITY ◆ NEW DELHI ◆ HONG KONG ◆ BUENOS AIRES

Credits

Pages 55 and 132: From *Still Learning to Read: Teaching Students in Grades 3–6* by Franki Sibberson and Karen Szymusiak. Copyright © 2003 by Franki Sibberson and Karen Szymusiak, with permission of Stenhouse Publishers.

Page 58: From *Developmental Reading Assessment Grades 4-8, Teacher Observation Guide.* Copyright © 2003 by Pearson Education, Inc., or its affiliate(s). Used by permission.

Page 94: Excerpt from "The Testing Tree." Copyright © 1968 by Stanley Kunitz from *Passing Through: The Later Poems New and Selected* by Stanley Kunitz. Used by permission of W. W. Norton & Company, Inc.

Page 94: From *The Miraculous Journey of Edward Tulane* by Kate DiCamillo. Text copyright © 2006 by Kate DiCamillo. Reprinted by permission of Candlewick Press, Inc., Cambridge, MA.

Pages 141–144: Excerpt from *Replay* by Sharon Creech. Copyright © 2005 by Sharon Creech. Used by permission of HarperCollins Publishers.

Page 150: Excerpt from *Gossamer* by Lois Lowry. Copyright © 2006 by Lois Lowry. Reprinted by permission of Houghton Mifflin Company. All rights reserved.

Excerpts from *Adolescent Literacy in Perspective*, November/December 2005, "Working Through Challenging Texts," appear throughout this book. http://www.ohiorc.org/adlit/in_perspective.aspx?id=179&status=0. Adapted with permission.

Editor: Raymond Coutu

Cover and interior design by Jorge J. Namerow

Photos by Flora Marlatt

Copy editor: Shelley Griffin

ISBN-13: 978-0-439-82132-2

ISBN-10: 0-439-82132-0

Copyright © 2008 by Franki Sibberson and Karen Szymusiak

All rights reserved. Published by Scholastic Inc.

Printed in the U.S.A.

2 3 4 5 6 7 8 9 10   40   13 12 11 10 09 08

Table of Contents

Acknowledgements

"I would be most content if my children grew up to be the kind of people who think decorating consists mostly of building enough bookshelves."

—Anna Quindlen, *How Reading Changed My Life (1998)*

Imagine if children designed our schools. Would they create grand rooms filled with books from floor to ceiling? Would they create comfortable places to gather with other readers to talk about books they are reading? Would they treasure long blocks of time to dig deeply into the words on the page? Would they uncover layers of meaning between the lines? Would children embrace characters they met in books as though they were long-lost friends who found their way home? We can hope they would.

We are the architects of our classrooms and of the conversations that happen in our learning lives, but we cannot accomplish our best work alone. We must listen to the voices of our students and build upon what we come to know about them. If we sit alongside them in classrooms filled with books, our students inspire us to imagine ways to build thoughtful school communities.

And so it was when we first began to write this book. We listened to our students and we watched their reading lives unfold before us. They are the first ones we thank because we continue to learn so much from them. They give us a reason to imagine the possibilities.

We are fortunate to be a part of the Dublin City Schools. We have grown as professionals because we have worked with thoughtful colleagues throughout our careers. The culture of learning and teaching in Dublin is the foundation for our work with children.

Ray Coutu, our editor at Scholastic, has encouraged us beyond our expectations. He guided us through the vision for this book and helped us learn so much about our own teaching and writing. His patience is quite remarkable. He never wavered in his belief that we could actually do this. Others at Scholastic have also been supportive. A huge thank-you to Lois Bridges, Terry Cooper, Susan Kolwicz, and Jorge Namerow. We'd also like to thank Laura Robb for her encouraging words when we thought we weren't going to be able to finish.

Our good friends Ralph Fletcher, Mary Lee Hahn, Jen Morgan, Brenda Power, Jill Reinhart, and Josie Stewart listened tirelessly during the writing of this book. We would never have made it past the first draft without Jill Reinhart. She read and responded in ways that helped us bring our thoughts into focus. A special thank-you to Flora Marlatt for taking such amazing photographs for the cover and interior.

Nancie Atwell has inspired us with her dedication to the reading and writing lives of children. We have learned so much from her that has influenced our work. We admire her commitment to authentic reading and writing workshops and are honored by the foreword she has written.

And finally, we would like to thank our families. This book seemed to take over our lives for a little while and they never stopped giving us their support. They understand that learning, teaching, and writing are a part of who we are. Knowing that they believe in our work with children makes it all worthwhile.

Foreword

The idea of teaching reading in a workshop can seem an unnerving prospect: *You mean, you just have them read? That's it?* Of course, reading—and loving—books is the heart of the workshop. But if students are to live as readers, they'll need teachers who do, too—teachers who are intimate with great children's literature, appreciative of it, and knowledgeable about the ways that young readers grow. Good reading workshop teachers know how to observe kids, how to ask questions about their processes and practices, and how to make sense of these data, both to inform their teaching and to describe their students' progress. Franki Sibberson and Karen Szymusiak are outstanding reading workshop teachers.

Day-to-Day Assessment in the Reading Workshop is the invaluable account of how Franki embeds assessment in the work and play of her intermediate-level workshop. The grades between 3 and 6 are a critical but insufficiently studied time of transition for young readers, as they move from the abbreviated, illustrated texts of the primary years to extended chunks of prose—novels and other kinds of chapter books. Franki and Karen's long experience teaching at this level, combined with their smart insights about reading and readers, demonstrate how thoughtful, purposeful choices help transform  beginning readers into fluent, self-aware, *literary* readers. They detail the routines of reading workshop in grades 3 to 6 in the essential context of establishing an intellectual community in which every reader has a role. And, most significantly, they show and tell how effective assessment in a workshop setting is an integral part of the processes of teaching and learning reading.

Nothing that Franki does as a teacher of reading is arbitrary. Through mini-lessons, read-alouds, independent reading, and small-group collaborations, students learn how to pay attention to their choices, habits, responses, confusions, behaviors, and preferences.

The children's self-awareness is a strong foundation for assessment. Because their tastes and intentions are taken seriously, her students easily engage with issues of what makes sense and what's significant, and she easily engages with their ideas, processes, and growth as readers.

Franki and Karen detail a range of evaluative data, from patterns to look for to questions and systems that illuminate a young reader's strengths and challenges. Their approaches invite teachers to recognize and support a student's genuine progress, as opposed to charting the minutiae of a checklist from a prepackaged program. The evidence they gather is specific, objective, and *heartening*: rather than merely prepping kids for the next standardized test, they are building strong, passionate readers for a lifetime.

Franki and Karen conclude that "everyone has a place to grow in the reading workshop." I think that this is the ultimate argument in favor of a workshop approach to teaching reading—and writing, too. The workshop is the best, maybe the only, *truly* differentiated approach to teaching and learning. Here, students act as and are known as individuals. Here, teachers recognize and support the needs and growth of individual students. With clarity and conviction, *Day-to-Day Assessment in the Reading Workshop* shows intermediate-grade teachers how to engage with and reflect on the patterns and the idiosyncrasies in every child's life as a reader.

> " The workshop is the best, maybe the only, *truly* differentiated approach to teaching and learning. Here, students act as and are known as individuals. Here, teachers recognize and support the needs and growth of individual students. "

Nancie Atwell
Center for Teaching and Learning
Edgecomb, Maine

Introduction

> " Let us, with the ancient doctors, vow first to do no harm, and promise to resist measures that deprive children of their natural enthusiasm and exuberance as learners, their impulse to ask questions, to figure things out, to wonder, to express, to investigate, to construct, to imagine. Let us commit to a quiet contemplation of the idea that children are universally passionate learners. "
>
> —Robert L. Fried, *The Passionate Learner* (2002)

In an authentic reading workshop, students live their lives as readers and thinkers. They learn together as a community and share the joy of reading. Each day, students broaden their experiences with texts and develop new skills for understanding. Reading workshop is a place where students can become passionate readers.There's a place for every kind of learner in the reading workshop. So when we launch the reading workshop, we initiate routines that support a variety of learners. Everyone has a place to grow in the reading workshop. Our goal is to support that growth.

Knowing our students is critical to our work in the reading workshop. As teachers we make instructional decisions that support readers because we know these readers well. Assessment is a key to building our knowledge. We gather a variety of evidence, watch for changes in thinking, examine artifacts, and listen carefully to the insights students have about their own reading process.

Assessment has come to the forefront of the political landscape. With new standards, grade-level state tests, and accountability measures, we question whether our priorities are moving in the right direction. Instead of looking at what our students *can* do and scaffolding them as they move forward, standards, tests, and measures are forcing us to use a deficit model of assessment—and we wind up focusing on what kids *can't* do.

We've written this text to turn the tide. What we learn about in the context of reading workshop enables us to match students to the learning experiences they need to be successful. We are always on the lookout for the leaps in learning so we can build on what students *can* do. We uncover the intricate layers of their reading lives, design the level of support they need, and explicitly reach out to them as readers to guide them toward independence.

In the pages that follow, we describe the reading workshop and the consistent routines that we initiate. We explore the many opportunities we have for assessment and how the results of these assessments help us build scaffolds to move students toward independence. We examine how what we learn about students impacts our teaching. We share our conversations with students and how those interactions help students build meaning and become more thoughtful readers.

We have structured the book around the components of our reading workshop. First, we look closely at ways the routines of a reading workshop

Day-to-Day Assessment in the Reading Workshop

support day-to-day assessment. We share our thinking about the unique learning needs of students in grades 3 to 6. We consider the important work we undertake during the first six weeks of school because we know how critical this time is for our reading workshops to be effective. We look closely at implementing each routine, the assessment opportunities it provides, and examples of how that plays out in our classrooms. We end the book with a chapter on strategies for taking advantage of the natural times for assessment of individual student learning and the growth of the entire class.

Chapter 1

Assessment-Informed Instruction in the Reading Workshop, Grades 3–6

> " Every time I talk to the children I am learning about them. I like the words 'learning about' much more than I like 'assessing.' I learn about my children. I get to know them. I want to know *what* they know. I want to know *how* they know. Isn't that what assessment is all about—learning what children know? "
>
> —Jill Ostrow, *A Room With a Different View (1995)*

Good teaching begins with knowing our students. We can teach wisely and well when we have taken the time to understand them, think about what they need, and plan ways to move them toward independence. We need to know them as learners and as human beings. And, of course, as teachers of reading, we also need to know them as readers.

Coming to Know Readers in Grades 3 to 6

In the primary grades, children are easily supported by texts and guided by teachers to move from emergent to early readers. Books for emerging readers offer plenty of support with patterned texts and strong visuals. Primary teachers provide clear introductions to the texts and scaffolds to support understanding. They poise their students for success by modeling and guiding them through the process of reading. They move from actively contributing to the reading process to gradually providing less support so their students can become more independent. But as children transition into the intermediate grades, they take on new characteristics as readers and learners. They develop interests and gather life experiences that impact their learning. They become more independent in their learning and develop a timeline of reading experiences on their way toward becoming proficient readers of a variety of texts. If they are motivated and engaged, this is a time when they can sharpen their learning styles and develop strategies for problem solving and higher-order thinking. With plenty of encouragement, support, and collaboration, they can develop a strong sense of efficacy that will promote lifelong learning. Children in grades 3 to 6 need to believe that they can be responsible for their own learning, that they can make choices in their learning, and that they can and should reflect on their progress. In every respect, they need to know that they are active and responsible learners, with peers and adults who support them. As Peter Johnston (2004) reminds us, "If nothing else, children should leave school with a sense that if they act, and act strategically, they can accomplish their goals" (p. 29).

Students in the intermediate grades begin to encounter more complex texts. There are so many components of texts that challenge intermediate readers. They encounter formats that require them to think in new ways. They have to be able to recognize the cues in the text. Often a lapse in time or foreshadowing can confuse them. More than one story line can get in the way of their understanding unless they are able to recognize signal words. Metaphors can confound literal readers. Compared to primary texts, intermediate texts require readers to use much more sophisticated strategies.

Primary Texts		Intermediate Texts
contain strong visual cues	⟶	contain few or no visual cues
have simple sentence structure	⟶	have complex sentence structures
are simple and brief	⟶	are information laden
include few characters	⟶	include many characters
feature one or two settings	⟶	constantly shift settings
can be read in one session	⟶	take days or weeks to read
contain a simple format	⟶	have a challenging format

We cannot prepare students in grades 3 to 6 for every challenge they will encounter in the books they read. Our goal shifts from preparing them for *a* text to preparing them for *any* text. That means we need to help students build a repertoire of strategies. And we need to help them recognize when to use which strategies. To do that, we need to understand students well enough to provide support when it is needed and to back off when they are ready to take responsibility for their learning.

So much has been written about literacy development in the primary grades, middle school, and high school. However, literacy in grades 3 to 6 seems to be less popular in professional literature. But if we look at where our students are coming from in grades K to 2 and where they are going in grades 7 to 9, we can see how critical grades 3 to 6 are to literacy development.

Classroom Community for Readers

Intermediate students need a predictable, literate-rich environment just as much as primary students do. They need a classroom community that encourages risk taking, collaboration, independence, and reflection. Being part of such a community prepares them to step out and explore the many texts that are available to them. As teachers, we need to observe, listen, and assess so we understand their learning process and plan instructional routines that support them in their journey toward becoming proficient readers of a variety of texts. In her book *Our Last Best Shot: Guiding Our Children Through Early Adolescence*, Laura Sessions Stepp tells us, "For a child to learn what he loves to do, he first has to find out what is possible. He must be exposed to new places, people, and ideas and encouraged to try new activities he has never tried and to hone newfound skills" (2000, p. 28). So, when we think about our reading workshops in grades 3 to 6, we want our students to see themselves as readers and recognize the possibilities in reading and in books. To make this happen, we establish big, yearlong student goals.

We've spent time reading *Classics in the Classroom: Designing Accessible Literature Lessons* (Jago, 2004); *I Read It, but I Don't Get It: Comprehension Strategies for Adolescent Readers* (Tovani, 2000); *Deeper Reading: Comprehending Challenging Texts, 4 –12* (Gallagher, 2004); *The Literature Workshop: Teaching Texts and Their Readers* (Blau, 2003); and *Subjects Matter: Every Teacher's Guide to Content-Area Reading* (Daniels & Zemelman, 2004). We know that when our students

Our Yearlong Reading Goals for Students in Grades 3 to 6

◆ To see themselves as empowered readers

◆ To recognize the power of literature to understand life issues

◆ To see purposes for different types of reading

◆ To build a toolbox of strategies that will support them with any text they encounter

◆ To recognize that their thinking changes as they read

◆ To think beyond the surface level of texts and uncover a deeper meaning

◆ To reflect about their own reading processes

◆ To support all of their thinking about texts with evidence

◆ To analyze all forms of text to gain understanding

◆ To understand an author's intent in writing

leave us in the intermediate grades and move on to middle school then high school, they will encounter more sophisticated texts. They will be expected to read and understand material in all content areas. They will be asked to pull out information from nonfiction reading and to analyze literary elements in some of the classics. So, as teachers of readers in grades 3 to 6, we want to empower our students to be successful with all texts. We want our classroom community to support our students as they become independent and sophisticated readers of a variety of texts.

Authentic Learning in the Reading Workshop

We want the structure and routines of reading workshop to represent what real readers do. We want children to think about their identities as readers and know that what we ask them to do in

school is as authentic as what readers do outside of school. We want them to be engaged in their reading and to take responsibility for their own learning.

Recently, we read Robert L. Fried's *The Game of School: Why We All Play It, How It Hurts Kids, and What It Will Take to Change It* (2005), and it encouraged us to think hard about the kinds of schools we have created for our students and what we can do to help our children become passionate and independent learners. It confirmed our own thoughts about what schools have become and what we have always hoped school could be. Fried reminds us in *The Passionate Learner: How Teachers and Parents Can Help Children Reclaim the Joy of Discovery* (2002), "Children come to us as passionate learners. It's our charge to help them develop the disposition to sustain, over a lifetime, an openness to things worth knowing" (p. 270).

However, we worry that some students have become disengaged and spend their time doing what they think the teacher wants. We worry about the authenticity of life at school and about reading experiences that don't feel real. Fried confirmed our suspicion that children enter school with a curiosity and willingness to learn, but quickly drop it to play by the rules of the game. If they want to do well in school, they figure out what the teacher wants and are rewarded with good grades. As Fried warns us, "While the teacher worries about making sure she covers her curriculum, and students scan the blackboard to determine what material is likely to be on the test, *authentic learning*—defined as *students engaged in ideas, concepts, skills, and activities that mean something to them and that lead both to a deeper understanding and to the ability to put ideas to work*—gets pushed so far into the background that it all but disappears" (2005, p. x). It is sad to think that our children are getting better at the game of school and worse at understanding what it means to be a passionate learner. Without passion for learning, school becomes lifeless and unproductive.

According to Fried, what has become the norm in our schools is "unengaged compliance. Students become game players by reflex and learners only on occasion." It is frightening to think that children come to school expecting to play a passive role and be fed a steady stream of meaningless assignments and tasks instead of engaging in purposeful learning and discovery.

What are the implications for reading workshops? How can we create authentic reading workshops? What can we do to put the students in charge of their learning so they can become passionate learners? How can we motivate students to become inspired and engaged learners instead of game players? What routines can we establish that will lead to authentic learning?

To a large extent, the answers lie in the big messages embedded within the routines of our reading workshop and in the way we talk with our students. These big messages should reflect how much we value authentic learning, active participation in the learning process, and a sense of discovery. They should recognize and celebrate independent and authentic learning.

In this time of testing and standards, we often sacrifice the most authentic component of a reading workshop: time for reading independently. Because teachers are pressured to fit everything into a school day and have learned the importance of explicit instruction, we wonder if too much reading time is spent talking *at* students rather than *with* students. With the emphasis on guided reading and leveled books, we worry that children are learning to depend on their teacher to choose books for them and that they are not being shown how to choose books or given the opportunity to do so. With all of the packaged and scripted programs available, we worry that teachers rely on the programs instead of what they know about each student's needs as a reader and a learner.

We wrote *Beyond Leveled Books: Supporting Transitional Readers in Grades 2–5* (Szymusiak & Sibberson, 2001) because of a concern that leveled books seemed to be taking over our classrooms and our students' reading time. We certainly know the value of leveled books and were not advocating for their elimination, just for a less dominant presence in our students' reading lives.

Now we wonder about the quality of reading workshop. We've learned so much about the nature of learning, struggling readers, comprehension instruction, and fluency. Based on our new understandings, we have reinvented our reading workshops to effectively meet the needs of our students. It is critical that we protect the time, predictable structure, student ownership, and response in our reading workshop. It's what gives our students the foothold they need to become lifelong readers.

Launching a Reading Workshop

Franki taught first grade for three years and loved every minute of it. She loved how the children immersed themselves in books, reading, and learning to read. She loved the enthusiasm children brought to books and the excitement they felt when the text made sense to them. She implemented a reading and writing workshop and her students soared. Franki learned so much from these young readers, but she was ready for a new challenge. She wondered what older readers were like so she asked to be moved to a fourth-grade classroom the next fall. As much as she hated to leave those emerging readers, Franki was excited to teach and learn with older students.

That summer Franki was pregnant with her first child and hooked on Doritos. So, during that first week of summer vacation, while her husband was out delivering pizzas for some extra money, she sat on the couch in her apartment with *In the Middle: Writing, Reading, and Learning With Adolescents* (Atwell, 1987) in one hand and a bag of Doritos in the other. She read the book in two sittings. Franki was so excited that she immediately called her new fourth-grade colleague, Patty Carpenter, and told her that she needed to read it. That fall they launched a reading workshop that included so much of what they learned from Nancie Atwell, with lots of time for students to read books of their choice, mini-lessons to support them in their reading, and conferences to check in with individual students. The book helped Franki understand that she could immerse her fourth graders in reading just as she had done with her first graders.

It's hard for Franki to believe that it has been nearly 17 years since she implemented that first reading workshop. She's learned so much about reading and learning. In this section, we talk about the critical routines of a reading workshop and how they support young readers.

Flexible, open-ended routines allow all children to enter the workshop at their own level

Our Routines for Reading Workshop

- Independent Reading
- Read-Aloud
- Whole-Class Instruction: Mini-Lessons
- Small-Group Instruction During Independent Reading
- Individual Reading Conferences During Independent Reading
- Share Time

of understanding and skills. With routines, we can use assessments to meet student needs. At the beginning of the year we may not know our students as well as we would like, but we put the routines in place because they will support *all* students, regardless of their strengths and weaknesses as readers. And we know that each routine allows daily, embedded assessment. Each routine serves a different purpose, and the routines work together to help the whole reader. Although all routines are important, we find the level of importance of each varies from year to year. After initial assessments, we may find that we need to focus more work on independent reading so that we can move kids forward in their reading. Other years, students may be capable of independent reading early in the year but not able to talk comfortably about books, so we focus our work and time in that area. We carry out routines every day all year, but the extent to which a particular routine acts as the anchor for learning changes throughout the year. What we try to do is put many routines in place—activities that students are comfortable with that reflect authentic reading—and we build on those based on the assessments we conduct, both formal and informal.

How Reading Workshop Fits Into Our Day

Our students read and write throughout the school day. But they also have sufficient time to engage in content learning. Below is a typical daily schedule in a self-contained classroom.

8:50 – 9:15	**Nonfiction Reading Time, Poetry Friday!, Discovery Time (alternating days)**
9:15 –10:30	**Math**
10:30 –11:30	**Content Areas: Science, Social Studies, Health**
11:30 –12:15	**Writing Workshop**
12:15 –1:00	**Lunch and Recess**
1:00 – 2:20	**Reading Workshop:**
	Read-Aloud (1:00 –1:25)
	Mini-Lesson (1:25 –1:35)
	Independent Reading, Small-Group Instruction, and Individual Conferences (1:35 –2:15)
	Share Time (2:15 –2:20)
2:20 – 2:40	**Content Reading and/or Word Study**
2:40 – 3:30	**Related Arts: Music, Art, Physical Education**

Benefits of Reading Workshop

In *Teaching the Best Practice Way: Methods That Matter, K–12*, Harvey Daniels and Marilyn Bizar remind us of the value of reading workshop: "In this model, elementary and secondary classrooms are no longer merely locations where information is transmitted. Instead, they become working laboratories or studios, where genuine knowledge is created, real products are made, and authentic inquiry is pursued. The classroom workshop is the pedagogical embodiment of constructivist learning theory" (2004, p. 153). We believe this is true because of what the model affords students: time to read and write, a predictable structure, ownership of learning, and response to reading.

Time

Without time to read, our students cannot become better readers. For us, time for students to read is the most important part of our reading workshop. Our students come to expect that they will have extended blocks of time to read independently and with others. We want them to know that they will have time to think about the books they want to read and that we will support them in making book choices that are just right for them. A just-right book is not necessarily one that is at their appropriate reading level. If reading workshop is a time for students to develop into competent, well-rounded readers, there are many reasons a book may be just right for them.

Predictable Structure

On most days, students can count on time for read-aloud, a brief mini-lesson, independent reading time, and some type of sharing. They can also count on knowing that during independent reading time, we may pull together small groups for a particular purpose or request conferences with individual students. These clear expectations for reading workshop give students time to think about their own lives as readers, to plan for their own reading, and to recognize what they need as readers. The structure encourages them to develop responsibility for the learning that will happen each day.

Ownership of Learning

If students are to be lifelong readers, it is important that they own their learning and that they be given the opportunities in reading workshop to choose books and to plan for future reading. However, ownership means more than a choice of books. Ownership refers to students developing their identities as readers. We don't consider reading workshop a time to *prepare* them for living a life as a reader. The structure of the reading workshop allows our students to define and redefine themselves as readers.

Response to Reading

Responding is important both for students' growth as readers, and for assessment as well. Students need to give and receive responses to their reading lives. The routines we establish in the reading workshop promote a sense of collaboration as students and the teacher interact in response to the reading. Thinking about the books they are reading, the strategies they are using, and the behaviors they are learning are all part of response. Having places and routines for children to share their reading in authentic ways is a necessary part of the reading workshop. Students confer with the teacher and with one another. During the reading workshop, we gain critical information about students in the ways they respond. We consider what we discover about them and respond with support and explicitly designed instruction.

No matter what new understandings we develop about reading instruction, the foundations of time, predictable structure, ownership, and response never change because they encourage students to recognize their growth as readers. We know that reading workshops may look different from classroom to classroom. However, we strongly believe that for students to be engaged in an authentic reading workshop, these four characteristics cannot be sacrificed.

Assessment in the Reading Workshop

Assessing readers has always been difficult. Until recently, we teachers have often assigned questions, journal entries, or projects at the end of a reading. But that just tested a basic level of understanding. We now know there's more to reading and comprehension, and we cannot continue to carry out assessments as we had. If we give our students end-of-the-book questions, how does that inform our teaching? Does it give our students the message that we don't believe they have read the material unless they can answer the questions? Summative assessments like these don't really help us support our readers. Why wait until the end of the reading to assess, when listening, observing, and asking questions along the way will give us so much more information about our readers and inform our instruction? We need to establish routines that afford us opportunities to assess in the context of authentic reading and writing experiences. If we watch and learn from our students while they are in the process of reading, we can use that information to plan instruction more effectively.

Gathering Data About Students

We are learning about our students every minute of every school day. We observe behaviors, listen in on conversations, pay attention to responses to whole-class lessons, look closely at reading notebooks, and more. Using the information we gain, we are able to add to the profile we have of each student. No assessment we use is better than another, and none of them is strong enough to stand alone. Below are some of the assessments that we will be discussing throughout the book. We will mention them briefly here and will discuss them more thoroughly in subsequent chapters.

- Listening to conversations
- Observing
- Individual conferences
- Casual conversations throughout the day
- Reading interviews
- Reading logs
- Status of the class
- Read-aloud notebooks

Listening and Observing

We cannot easily separate assessment from teaching. We walk around the room listening in on conversations and glancing over students' shoulders so we can assess their learning. When we really listen to children, we learn so much about them and discover many opportunities to teach. The more we learn about them, the easier we can make our instructional decisions. Every conversation becomes a window into their learning.

Individual Conferences and Casual Conversations

We used to believe that what counted most were the teacher-student reading conferences. We used to rely on these conferences as checkpoints to judge whether the child had actually read and understood the book. Although these conferences gave us some information, we were actually more focused on the book than on the reader. We've changed our thinking about individual conferences.

We recognize the importance of the conferences, but we have come to see that the conversations we have with students throughout the day are also critical. We take notes during the reading workshop and listen to our students' responses in our conversations throughout the day. Each time we talk to a student, we gather new information. We rely on conversation—short and long, formal and informal—as a critical part of assessment.

Reading Interviews

Asking students questions about their lives as readers is a great way to create reader profiles, especially at the beginning of the school year. We prepare by thinking about what we want to know about our students. We also think about the messages our questions will send to students. The questions we ask must show them that we are interested in their lives as readers. We also want students to learn something about themselves and to begin to think about the questions we pose.

Reading Logs and Status of the Class

Our students keep track of their daily reading by maintaining reading logs. Students can also use the log for self-reflection as they look back to think about what they have been reading and look for patterns in their reading behaviors, and we can do the same.

We use the status of the class to quickly check at the beginning of the reading workshop what each child plans to do in reading each day. It gives us a view of each student's reading practices and provides opportunities for us to have brief conversations with students or plan for individual conferences during the reading workshop.

Read-Aloud Notebooks

We want our students to have a place to write and collect their thinking during our daily read-aloud. Each child has a spiral read-aloud notebook. We often stop during read-aloud and invite students to jot their thinking in their notebooks. The notebooks give us insight into the ways our students are thinking about their reading. We use information from them to help us guide conversations and plan future mini-lessons. An easy and nonthreatening way to assess notebooks is to sit alongside different students during the read-aloud time each day. We can then glance at their notebooks and see how they are using them.

Assessing the Whole Reader

Under the pressure of standardized testing, it is all too easy to look only at the numbers. But, if we really want to use what we know about our students to help them move forward, we need to look at all of the information that we have—qualitative and quantitative. By looking only at test scores, we ignore other important data. If we rely on a narrow perspective of assessment, we do a major disservice to children. Throughout this book we will share what we notice about our students and how we use these insights to plan instruction.

Every minute, every lesson, and every conversation can inform our teaching. We rarely give assignments for the sole purpose of assessing. Instead, we invite students to try a new strategy or a new way of thinking and watch them apply it. We think about how students can demonstrate what they know. Then we observe and assess them to determine their level of success.

Standards and Standards-Based Assessments

In our state, we have clearly defined standards for literacy development. In reading workshop, we include authentic ways for students to gain knowledge of the content, strategies, and skills in the reading standards. We create opportunities to measure the progress of students toward meeting the standards. However, many of the opportunities to assess within the reading workshop go far beyond what is expected in the standards. If we pay close attention to the children, they will show us much more about their lives as readers and learners. We observe the reading process in action and intervene at the most opportune times to encourage independence. So much of what we learn about the students helps us make moment-to-moment instructional decisions and respond in meaningful ways.

We have found that knowing the standards well is our best tool. We keep copies of our state standards handy and refer to them often. But instead of writing lessons so we can check off what standard we taught, we want to make sure to include much of that content into real conversations about books. We know that conversations are often the best and most authentic way to begin thinking about many of the standards. By knowing the state standards well, we can introduce words such as *theme* and *plot* in read-aloud discussions. We can create reflection sheets that help students become aware of the strategies they are using. We can introduce new ways of thinking about books that reflect the language of the standards. When we know the standards well, we can embed our standards teaching into the authentic work of students who are reading books and talking about their reading every day.

We administer some assignments, such as a survey or a two-column chart, at intervals throughout the school year. This periodic assessment allows us to see how the students approach the same type of assignment as the year progresses. We want to know that at each interval the students are using more sophisticated levels of thinking.

Concluding Thoughts

In the next chapter, we look at how we launch a reading workshop and introduce the routines that provide opportunities to assess students from moment to moment and day to day. Our most critical goal during the first six weeks is to get to know all that we can about our students. The routines we implement during the first six weeks provide us with many opportunities to identify what our students can do. When we start with what they know and can do, we unleash their potential to be sophisticated and independent readers.

Chapter 2

The First Six Weeks of School

> 66 These students deserve the slow, thoughtful beginning that will guarantee a year filled with all that is possible. 99
>
> —Joanne Hindley, *In the Company of Children (1996)*

On the last day of school a few years ago, Franki's fifth graders were reflecting on their year, talking about things they were looking forward to and things they would miss once the last bell rang. Jonathan said, "I am going to miss that we are never going to be all together, in this room, laughing and learning again." The class sighed in agreement.

We know our classrooms never feel quite the same from year to year. We know that different groups of students come together in different ways. We know that strategies that build community one year might not the next. But we adjust our teaching to ensure that community has an impact on students' learning and living.

The first six weeks are critical to the kind of class we will create each year. During that time, we give students messages about what it will be like to learn together all year. Our actions and words show students what we value and how learning happens. We build relationships, set routines, find out about one another, and discover how to live and learn together. The first six weeks offer a huge window of opportunity to get to know our students, as human beings first and then as learners. If we use this time well and begin to build a profile of each student, we can use what we learn to plan our instruction.

Reading workshop provides the perfect structure for getting to know our students each day in the classroom. During the routines of reading workshop, we observe each child. We begin to build a profile of each of our students as readers. This first six weeks marks the beginning of our yearlong profile of each student.

Creating an Intellectual Community

In the past, when speaking at workshops about the first six weeks, we focused almost exclusively on the importance of building community mainly to give students a chance to get to know one another. We knew that it was important for students to feel comfortable and valued in the classroom. We wanted them to feel part of a group, and we knew that we wanted them to build relationships with their classmates. We knew that if they were happy learning, the learning would be better.

However, we now know that building community for social reasons isn't enough. Our goal during those first weeks should be to build an *intellectual* community—one in which participants come together to learn, where everyone grows *because* of the community. It is important that we build a community where learning and growth are the goals, where everyone has a part to play, and where we are each more successful individually because of the entire group.

Building an intellectual community takes a bit more effort and patience than building a more traditional community. Students in grades 3 to 6 tend to come with preconceived notions about school. They come believing certain things about themselves and others. They are quick to identify classmates who find learning easy and those who struggle. They pinpoint who is "smart," who is "popular," and who is "trouble." It is important for us to minimize that thinking and help every child feel part of the intellectual community that we are creating. By assessing all day, every day to find our students' strengths, to give them ownership of their learning, and to help them see the value of themselves and others in the classroom, and sharing what we learn with them, we go a long way in eliminating preconceived notions.

We want our students to understand the power and potential of an intellectual community. We want them to know that we believe they each have something unique to add to our thinking. We want them to know that when one of them is absent, the community will feel a bit different because the group works and learns best when it is whole.

Our goal during the first six weeks is to initiate routines and begin to create profiles of students within an intellectual community. In this chapter, we consider the routines in the reading workshop, including independent reading, read-aloud, mini-lessons, small-group instruction, conferring, and sharing. We reflect on how we implement these routines. We also share ways that we gather information about each student and about the class as a whole during this critical time. We focus on how we structure the reading workshop to meet our goal by the end of the sixth week.

Sending Big Messages

Another important consideration is the big messages embedded within the learning routines that we initiate, such as the value of authentic learning, active participation in the learning process, and a sense of discovery. These messages should be invitations to celebrate both collaborative and independent learning.

Conveying these messages begins on the first day of school with the first words we utter and the initial conversations we have with children. It begins with the routines we carefully introduce and continues as we extend and revise those routines throughout the year. It is purposeful and meaningful planning in a classroom environment that supports curiosity, authentic learning, and thoughtful conversations.

We persist until we convince our students that they are an integral part of the learning process. We encourage them to ask questions, to reflect, and to be deep thinkers. We help them to become active learners. Some students have learned the game of school so well that it takes a while for them to understand that learning may be different in our classroom. But eventually, they come to recognize that they are part of a community of learners who depend on one another.

It is very tempting to speed things up early in the year so that we can begin to move toward our bigger goals. We've learned to have patience while our students find their identities as readers. We want children to stop playing the game of school, to recognize their role in the learning community, and to be excited about becoming independent learners. All of this takes time.

Teaching Content and Standards

Teaching content and the standards is important to us—very important—but we ease into it during the first six weeks. As a matter of fact, we try hard *not* to focus on skills and content. Instead, we teach about what reading means in this classroom and how conversation is valued. By standing back and watching, dropping questions, inviting student response, and initiating open-ended conversations, we begin to teach our students authentically. By starting the school year this way, children don't jump through hoops to make us happy. Instead they take responsibility for the learning process and participate in learning experiences. And we are focused on learning about each student by actively listening and participating in their learning.

Gathering Information About Our Students

For reading workshop to be successful, we need to start learning about individual students from the start of the year. Some information is gathered formally using standardized assessments, but most is gathered informally through reading interviews, observations, and conferences.

Through these assessments we learn so much about our students. In each routine, we watch and listen so we can begin a profile for each student and for the class as a whole. These profiles show us patterns of learning and patterns of challenges for individuals and the group. Knowing these patterns helps us teach wisely all year. Profiles change as we collect new information on our students. During each routine, we gather information about students, and each day we add detail to profiles and sharpen our focus.

Record-Keeping Tools for the First Six Weeks

- Sticky notes with observations/conversations
- Pages from reading notebook
- Status-of-the-class form
- Reading logs
- Record of comments during read-aloud

What We've Come to Know

Because we have been teaching a long time, we've come to know that there are some behaviors that are common to students this age, such as carrying around big, fat books that are far too hard for them. Having this experience helps us in our assessments. We certainly don't expect every child or every class to exhibit the same behaviors. But we know that the more experiences we have, the more we have to draw from. In her book *One Child at a Time: Making the Most of Your Time With Struggling Readers K–6*, Pat Johnson says, "We continually broaden and refine our understandings about reading process, about assessment matching instruction, and about teaching for strategies. What we discover from each new child we work with and each new problem we address adds layers to our knowledge base" (2006, p. 11).

Establishing Routines

Setting up routines during the first weeks is all about helping our students see possibilities in their literate lives. Each routine sends an important message about how we will work in the classroom and what reading can mean for students beyond the classroom. So we plan carefully for read-aloud, mini-lessons, independent reading, conferences, share, and small-group instruction.

Because time is scarce, we try not to waste a minute. That means that each routine has to support *every* reader, *every* day. We have to think about ways to meet the needs of our struggling readers as well as our more proficient readers. Our routines must help students overcome challenges and achieve. This begins with assessing them wisely and continuously.

Furthermore, our routines must be flexible enough to change as students become more independent in their reading. They have to provide an entry point for every student's unique strengths and weaknesses. Finally, they must help us look at the whole class and individual students at the same time.

What We Typically Discover Early in the Year

Students:

- Share oral retellings and responses that are stronger than written retellings and responses
- Believe that difficult, long books are best
- Think that "sounding out" is the best strategy
- Have difficulty sticking with books
- Have difficulty choosing books that are a good fit
- Often have good fluency, but poor comprehension
- Often have good comprehension, but poor fluency
- Are competitive when making predictions in read-aloud because they are too focused on "being correct"
- Read for plot only
- Often have a favorite author

Those are the challenges of establishing thoughtful, meaningful routines.

Routines can help students learn about themselves as readers and learners. When students are given opportunities to be reflective about their reading lives, they develop more responsibility for determining what they need each day in the reading workshop.

Independent Reading

Independent reading time is the most critical routine of reading workshop. During independent reading, students read books of their choice for a sustained period of time (30 to 45 minutes per day). Our goal for the first several weeks is to build stamina. Small-group work, individual conferences, literature discussions, and other reading activities also happen during this time. But we also make sure that every child has large blocks of uninterrupted reading time each week.

Independent reading time on that first day of school is always a surprise. Even for children who have read all summer, getting back into the routine of reading in a new classroom with new classmates and a new teacher takes time. It takes trust and patience. But it is so important in helping students get into the habit of reading and providing us with a way of getting baseline information about them. Some teachers may start with a shorter time for independent reading, but it's critical to build on that time each day until students can read independently for at least 30 minutes. To do this, we must make expectations clear and make sure students choose just-right books.

> ## Big Messages We Send During Independent Reading
>
> ◆ People choose books for various reasons.
> ◆ An individual's tastes and mood are important when choosing books.
> ◆ There are people in the classroom who can recommend books to you.
> ◆ Knowing others as readers can help you grow as a reader.
> ◆ Finding books that you can read and enjoy from start to finish is important.
> ◆ People sometimes choose a book because they've read others like it.
> ◆ Keeping track of what you read helps with future reading.
> ◆ People have a variety of thoughts while reading.
> ◆ Reflecting on your own reading is important to your growth as a reader.

Early in the year, we give students 10 to 15 minutes, which is just enough time for them to become engaged without losing attention and staring at the clock. We want students to be comfortable and relaxed. We want them to have enough to read for the entire 15 minutes. By holding students accountable for staying seated with books for this brief time, we are teaching them how reading workshop will feel each day. Over time, they will improve their stamina and read for longer periods.

Working with students individually, we make sure they are engaged in just-right books and know what we expect of them. We communicate these important messages:

- Individual preference is important.
- The teacher is interested in who I am as a reader.
- The teacher and my classmates know good books that I might enjoy.
- Knowing myself as a reader can help me grow as a reader.
- Previewing will help me choose good books.

Our role is critical during the first six weeks. It often feels like we are spinning plates for weeks, trying to help students find the right books, stick with books, and build stamina. Talking about books and book choice takes up a great deal of time. But students cannot grow as readers if they are not engaged, do not enjoy reading, or do not see themselves as readers. So we are always on the lookout for students whose minds wander during independent reading time. We work to identify what is keeping them from being engaged and building stamina. We ask ourselves these questions:

- Are they choosing books that are appropriate?
- Do they know the kinds of books they like?
- Do they have trouble sticking with a book until the end?
- Do they wander around the room during independent reading time?
- Do they have favorite authors, genres, or series?

As Lucy Calkins reminds us in *The Art of Teaching Reading* (2000), "Once you really pull in close to consider children's understandings (and misunderstandings), it quickly becomes clear that 'simply' giving children time to read, texts they can understand, and conversations that hold them accountable to the text is a gigantic thing. An absolutely mind-blowing number of skills are needed and developed by anyone who reads with engagement and interest" (p. 357). We want our students to be reading books they enjoy and to be able to stick with the book until they are finished. We know that the first step for all children is getting into books.

Observation During Independent Reading

For the first several days of independent reading, we don't administer assessments in the traditional sense. Instead, we watch, listen, and learn about what students do in the routines. This is an important time for informal assessments. This work is so informative. For example, we may learn that a few children are struggling and others are quite secure in their reading. We try to notice as much as we can about our new students, including the following:

The Kind of Book Each Child Chooses to Read

- Haylie had a stack of books that were thick and difficult.

- Alyssa chose picture books that we read to the class.
- Conner was comfortable with nonfiction books that had lots of photos.
- Madelyn had a book in a series that she had been reading.
- Alex read *Boxcar Children*.
- Brennen brought all of his books from home and had no interest in books from the classroom library.

The Level of Engagement of Each Child

- Jonathan got up to use the restroom at least once each day during independent reading time.
- Shannon looked engaged but finished books very quickly.
- Matt got up to get tissues and drinks of water often.

The Location Each Child Chooses to Read

- Jessica always found a spot by herself and started reading.
- Kai seemed to like to read near friends. He often stopped to share something with a friend he was sitting near.

The Extent to Which Each Child Sticks With Books Over Several Days

- Carly quit several books during the first few days.
- Brennen finished a Magic Treehouse book during the first week.

The extent to which each child browses books thoughtfully

- Maggie chose books very quickly by looking at the cover.
- Sam seemed to be looking for something in particular on the shelves.

We need to avoid making big judgments about students' reading during the first few weeks. Rather, we need to watch for patterns, ask ourselves new questions, and get to know children the best we can by observing them in the process of reading. After we have observed them for several weeks, we can compile the information and plan instruction more effectively.

Reading Logs

Students use a reading log to write for a few minutes each day about their independent reading. At the beginning of the year, we often use a log similar to the one shown on the next page. These logs are on separate sheets of paper so that we can collect and analyze them as we build profiles of each student. Later these logs will change to something more focused on the child's individual goals. But for now, we want to see what happens when they can respond to

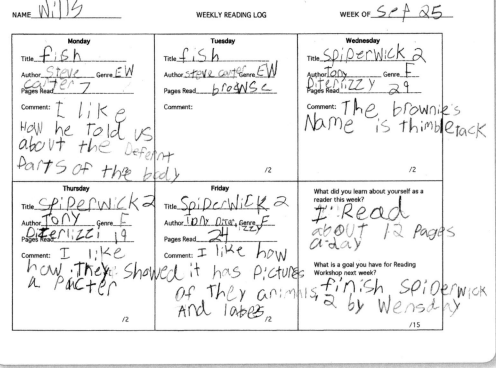

WEEKLY READING LOG

NAME Shivani   WEEK OF Sept./25

Monday	Tuesday	Wednesday
Title Stink	Title Spiderwick	Title Spiderwick
Author Megan Mcdonald Genre F	Author Arthur Spiderwick Genre Fantasy	Author Arthur Spiderwick Genre F
Pages Read 24	Pages Read 20	Pages Read 20
Comment: I like how the author talked about one thing and then talked about about another and then went back to the other things.	Comment: I like how in each book the author explains about a magical creature in each book	Comment: I do not have any
/2	/2	/2

Thursday	Friday	What did you learn about yourself as a reader this week?
Title Spiderwicks	Title Mary-kate and Ashley	I make more predictions.
Author Arthur Spiderwick Genre F	Author Judy Katsche Genre realistic F	
Pages Read 25	Pages Read 28	What is a goal you have for Reading Workshop next week?
Comment: I like how whenever the author introduces a new creature he would draw a picture of it	Comment: I like how the author keeps on making us guess what happens next.	I do not have any.
/2	/2	/15

WEEKLY READING LOG

NAME Wills   WEEK OF Sep 25

Monday	Tuesday	Wednesday
Title fish	Title fish	Title Spiderwick 2
Author Steve carter Genre EW	Author steve carter Genre EW	Author Tony Diterlizzy Genre F
Pages Read 7	Pages Read browsc	Pages Read 29
Comment: I like How he told us about the Deferent Parts of the body	Comment:	Comment: The brownie's Name is thimbletack
	/2	/2

Thursday	Friday	What did you learn about yourself as a reader this week?
Title Spiderwick 2	Title Spiderwick 2	I Read about 12 Pages a day
Author Tony Diterlizzi Genre F	Author Tony Diter izzy Genre F	
Pages Read 19	Pages Read 24	What is a goal you have for Reading Workshop next week?
Comment: I like how they Showed it has a Pacter	Comment: I like how of they animis And labes	finish Spiderwick 2 by Wensday
/2	/2	/15

These are student reading logs from one week during the first month of school. Although both students talk about what they like in the book, one student is focused on content while the other is more focused on the author's craft. Both students bounced between books. One student read nonfiction while the other seems comfortable with early chapter books. Goal setting and reflections were simple.

anything that seems important to them. They are free to write whatever they choose—perhaps a note on why they chose the book, where they decided to read, connections to other things they've read. At the end of each week, students answer two questions in their logs:

- What did you learn about yourself as a reader?
- What goal do you have for next week's independent reading?

The logs serve two purposes. First, they provide us with a glimpse of how students are using their time and what they think about their reading. We can quickly see when students start a new book. We can see the types of responses students write when given little or no direction. We can identify the kinds of goals they are setting. We can note how they write about themselves as readers.

Second, reading logs allow students to be in charge of their own reading lives and to set goals accordingly. If they did not have these logs, we would be the ones to say, "Joey, you quit three books today. You need to stick with one next week." Instead, the log is a tool to help students make discoveries like these on their own.

We collect the information from logs in many ways. We look over students' shoulders as they are writing. We often read them to get a sense of how the whole class is progressing. We lead whole-class conversations based on reflections from reading logs.

During the first six weeks, we help students who are having difficulty reading to build their identities as readers. We need to allow them to act like readers even if they don't see themselves as readers. We always have some students who pretend to read, but we know that will change. We are comfortable with children choosing books that are not necessarily right for them (too easy, too hard, not interesting) because we are confident they'll make wiser choices over time. For example, Franki noticed that Kelsie was busy with long, hard books, but her eyes wandered often and she didn't actually seem to be reading. At this point in the year, Franki didn't want to interfere because she knew from experience this issue would resolve itself in the first few weeks. Franki continued gathering information about Kelsie. When Kelsie exhibited behaviors like these, Franki knew that she needed to find a way to place value on easier, less demanding books. We are giving students big messages about their role in the reading workshop and letting them know that we see them as readers. The less we control students' reading, the more we can watch and learn about who they are as readers.

> ## What We Look for in Reading Logs
>
> - What kinds of comments are students making about the book?
> - Are they finishing books?
> - Are they reading a single book over several days or bouncing around?
> - Which genre do they seem to be reading?
> - Are they thoughtful about their book choice?
> - Do they set goals? What kinds of goals do they set?
> - How do they see themselves as readers?

Read-Aloud

Students are often unaware of the power they have as readers and the opportunities to be thinkers that books provide them. So it is important to have a time when it is safe to talk about those opportunities. For us, that's read-aloud time. Read-aloud not only provides many opportunities for modeling reading behaviors, it also invites students to talk through their understanding of the text and to build comprehension skills. Students learn from one another as well as the teacher, helping to build the intellectual community that's so important in the first six weeks.

Big Messages We Send During Read-Aloud

- Talking and writing are important ways to refine your thinking about reading.
- Everyone has something different to bring to the read-aloud and we can combine our thinking to gain new insights.
- There are many ways to respond to a book.
- We can chart our thinking to develop our understanding about how and what we read.
- We can use features in the text to boost our understanding.
- Putting our ideas together creates new thinking.

During read-aloud time, Franki and her students sit in a big circle on the floor. This allows everyone to see one another and supports group conversation. Because we use nonfiction in many other parts of the day, we often choose to read fiction during read-aloud time. We read the story aloud while students listen. On occasion, we give students copies of the book so they can mark certain pages with a sticky note or look back to clarify their thinking. However, we do this only when we feel that students will benefit from it. Otherwise we fear students will focus on following along, which can hinder comprehension for some.

Read-aloud is a time when we can help students see the possibilities in books. Primary students typically read a story for plot and focus on what is happening. They learn to recognize the beginning, middle, and end. They learn to identify the problem and the solution. But as students become more sophisticated in their reading, they encounter more complex books and stories that have layers of meaning. So, as teachers in grades 3 to 6, we must choose books for read-aloud that will benefit all of the readers in our class. For example, for students who are still struggling with understanding story structure, holding a story in their head over days, and keeping track of characters, we would choose a book with a clear, traditional plotline. But the book would also need to have an interesting theme or sophisticated elements to appeal to the more advanced readers. The books we choose should allow every child to enter and respond in ways that help them grow as readers.

Early in the year, we pick light, high-interest books for read-aloud so children look forward to this time of day. On the next page is a list of books that Franki has chosen for read-aloud at the beginning of the school year and her reasons for choosing them.

Favorite Read-Aloud Books for the Beginning of the Year

Frindle by Andrew Clements

Andrew Clements has written several books for students in grades 3 to 6. Franki often reads one of his books early in the year because they are easy to talk about. They feature strong characters involved in real-life issues—typically children who make decisions. Children always feel comfortable talking about Clements's books, and Franki hopes that by reading one aloud early in the year, many students will go on to read more of his books. To encourage this, Franki shares other books by him.

The Bad Beginning by Lemony Snicket

This is a great read-aloud for several reasons. The plot is interesting and students become quickly engaged in it and can make predictions quickly. Since it is the first book in a series, it introduces children to a range of books they may want to read in the future. The story contains layers of meaning, so Franki is never sure where the talk will go—it's a great way to open the door to the many ways of talking about a book.

The City of Ember by Jeanne DuPrau

The literary analysis students will be doing as the year goes on calls for supporting their thinking with evidence from the text. The detailed table of contents in this book helps students find support for their assertions about the text. Students are often comfortable making predictions, so Franki hangs an enlarged copy of the table of contents on the board in the read-aloud space. As they read aloud, students use the table of contents to support their predictions. It also helps them see how features in the text, such as a table of contents, can support them as they think through the book.

Instead of reading a book aloud and asking students to listen passively, we encourage them to explore the possibilities in the text by participating in discussion and writing activities. When read-aloud time is participatory, and the students are comfortable giving things a try, they can discover so much about an author's meaning. They can listen deeply and recognize themes that sophisticated readers recognize and understand the larger meaning the text has to offer.

Read-aloud is no longer what we do just after recess to calm the children into compliance. It is no longer reading through the text without stopping to talk about the story, theme, format, or strategies we use to make sense of the text. Instead, it is an interaction between the text, the teacher, and the children. It is a collaboration of thought that provides a foundation for future reading. It lays the groundwork for future conversations about other texts. It gives students a tool for making sense of texts they are reading independently or in small groups.

> ## Assessment During Read-Aloud
>
> Questions we ask ourselves:
>
> - Which students are comfortable jumping into the conversation?
> - Which students need an invitation to join the conversation?
> - Who is commenting about plot? about character? about theme?
> - Are students able to respond to others' comments or are they waiting to share their own thoughts instead?
> - What types of ideas are the students wondering about?
> - Are they engaged while the book is being read?
> - Are they engaged in the talk?

Early every year, Franki has a student who says he or she doesn't like the book she is reading or that he or she doesn't like to talk or write during read-aloud time. It is very tempting to give that "teacher look." However, those honest comments are valuable, especially during the first few weeks. Our response can send one of two messages to students: "We must agree with the teacher in this classroom" or "We will be heard and taken seriously in this classroom." There is no rule that every student must love every read-aloud book. A very interesting discussion often stems from why we like or do not like a certain book. In fact, a discussion like that helps us meet our goal of helping students understand that everyone has different tastes as a reader.

Contrary comments also teach us about the child who says them. If children complain about the talk that goes on in read-aloud time, it tells us that the talk is not working for them. It tells us that they are not engaged in the talk or that they aren't sure how the talk can help their thinking grow. Every comment becomes an opportunity for us to learn about individual students, as well as the whole group. Our response is one more piece of information that tells students how we will think and interact throughout the year.

Our goal is to empower students to read, not to teach them everything about the book we are reading aloud. By involving them in the conversation, we help them develop the skills necessary to think through text.

Strategies for Thinking and Understanding

Two of the most important tools students use are book previewing and read-aloud notebooks. Both help students with their independent reading. As with all of the tools and strategies, they support readers regardless of their level of proficiency. Both of these tools also serve as assessments by providing windows into student thinking.

Book Previewing

To set the stage for deep reading, we spend time previewing each new read-aloud book. Previewing serves many purposes early in the year:

- To teach students how to choose appropriate books
- To support comprehension with predictions
- To discover threads of thinking
- To give students a way to support their thinking with evidence in the text
- To start conversations
- To encourage students to attend to various features of a book that support comprehension

When we think about our own reading, we know we spend hours in a bookstore previewing to choose the right book. Before we even start to read the book, previewing gives us an idea of how the story will begin, where the story will go, the setting, and the characters. Likewise, previewing can help students comprehend better by familiarizing them with the characters, the setting, and other components of the story before they start to read. Since we do not usually have multiple copies of the book, we compile a "preview packet" for each student, made up of information-rich parts of the book (the cover, the epigraph, the back-cover blurb, the author blurb, the first page, the dedication, any maps or character charts). For the first few read-aloud previews, we preview together, looking at each piece of the preview and noting all that we know and can predict about the book before beginning to read it. After the preview, we ask students to list the questions they've come up with. The preview and the questions set the stage for thoughtful discussions for the entire book.

Early in the year, most students have not had experience previewing, so the preview activity is often about things they notice and might predict. We try to push the conversation along by asking, "What makes you think that?" each time a child makes a prediction. This helps all students begin to support their predictions with thinking and evidence from the text—an important skill for students moving toward independence in their reading.

Previewing meets different needs for different students. For students who are just beginning to read chapter books, it supports comprehension by giving them background into the story. Students who are at more sophisticated levels use the preview to think through the possibilities, to predict themes, and to find threads of thinking to follow as they read. Previewing also provides us with information and insight about each child.

- What *do* they notice with the preview?
- Do they make reasonable predictions?
- Do they use prior knowledge about books?

Previewing is the strategy that transfers most quickly and visibly to independent reading time because the initial goal of previewing is to help students choose appropriate books. But that's only one goal of previewing. We also watch for other previewing behaviors:

- Using preview pages throughout the read-aloud to reread and rethink
- Talking during reading conferences about how the preview helped them understand the text
- Talking to others after the preview—making good predictions about the book

Students and teacher sit in a circle on the floor during read-aloud.

Read-Aloud Notebooks

During read-aloud time, our students jot down their thinking in read-aloud notebooks at key stopping points. We may also give them time to talk as a group to put their ideas together and write them down. The read-aloud notebook is a safe place for readers to use writing as a means to think more deeply about the text. We don't give much direction. We simply ask students to write down whatever they are thinking. This allows us to see the ways students naturally respond to text. It helps us to see who is a risk taker and who is worried about "getting it right." By keeping the process open-ended, we help students go beyond simple ideas and think in abstract ways.

We also use the notebooks to learn about students. In her class, Franki looks for variety in her students' notebooks. If we consider the four samples below, we can see how she applied what she learned to the whole class to improve the reading of all students. These four students responded in different ways during the first few days of read-aloud. We learn so much by looking at each sample.

We see a child who is comfortable with predictions. He writes a prediction each time he reads. We can move him forward by encouraging him to support his predictions.

Shredder man
I predict that Nolan will stop Bubba from being a bully.
I predict that Nolan's Plan will Work.
I predict that Nolan becomes Shreddman.
I predict that someone will go on Nolan A.K.t. shredderman. on. I think Mr. green will tell Dr. Voss
I predict

"Shredder man 9\6\06"
"I theak that nose is going to make the web of Shredderman big."
"9\8\06"
"Shredder man"
"9\11\06"
"9\12\06"
"bubba is going to be tured diffrint kid. 9\13\06"
"mr. green is not a Side kick. 9\13\06"
"I think mr. Bixbe is going to be mean"

For students who are clearly sticking with one type of response because it is safe, it is important that we value their response to build their confidence. We do that by bringing that response to the whole class as a way to expand others' notebook entries.

Early in the year, students are often focused on understanding the plot, making predictions, and summarizing. But as the year goes on, children discover new ways to keep track of their thinking, as they become more sophisticated readers and thinkers.

People often ask us if we grade read-aloud notebooks. The answer is an unequivocal no because we want the notebooks to be tools for thinking. Our goal is not for a notebook to be filled up, but rather that students see how writing can help them clarify their thoughts about text. In Chapter 4, we discuss ways we assess students' use of the read-aloud notebook across the school year.

We see another child who is comfortable summarizing. The summaries are solid and do give a sense of the main events in each chapter. This child seems able to follow plot. She is safe in her responses. We can encourage her to try different types of responses.

I'm an old - oh my gosh!

9.1

Ch. 1 Bubba Bixby - Bubba is a bully. he steals, has killer breath, hogs the ball in 4 □, name caller, has rocky knuckles.

Ch. 2 Mr. Green Homework Machine - Mr. Green made a Home

Ch.3 Spy Tools - Nolan is planning to spy on Bubba. He put a camra on the back of his book bag.

Ch. 4 Level 42-E — At the Pledge of alligence Bubba cut off a peice of Mariam's hair.

Mr. Greens class had a test. Nolan got 100% and Mr. Green wrote that Nolan shreds!

Ch.5 Secret identidy - Nolan first missed the Picture but on friday he got a picture.

Nolan wants to make a website to put his project on and he wants a secret identedy on the website. The website is www.shredderman.com

Whole-Class Instruction: Mini-Lessons

Mini-lessons in the reading workshop are quick, focused, and powerful. They give us opportunities to teach explicitly. They also give us opportunities to help students think about themselves as readers and to begin to talk about their reading lives. Early mini-lessons fall into the following categories:

- ◆ Expanding students' definitions of reading
- ◆ Understanding procedures for reading workshop
- ◆ Learning to talk about books effectively
- ◆ Beginning to know themselves as readers

Shredderman
Level 42-E

Shredder man was in Level 42-E
that is a really high level
He has the highest Level in
the class. Mr. Green said to
Nollen "you shred man."

I think that Bubba's mean
friends (Bullys with Bubba)
gets the camera from Nolen.

Secret Identity

- Nolan is going to make a
website about Bubba on
the computer.

Many of the mini-lessons during the first six weeks of school focus on book choice and reader identity. We often use short text so we can introduce many ways for students to respond to books. Because independent reading time is often shorter during the first few weeks of school, we have a bit more time for mini-lessons. During these first six weeks, our mini-lessons are about 20 minutes long. But as the year progresses and students become more proficient, we devote less time to mini-lessons and more to independent reading.

> **Big Messages We Send During Whole-Class Instruction**
>
> ◆ Knowing who you are as a reader helps you move forward.
>
> ◆ There are many ways to think about a text as you are reading it.
>
> ◆ Paying attention to your thinking during reading is important.
>
> ◆ You can do many things to help yourself when you are stuck.
>
> ◆ A text may be hard or easy, depending on the reader.
>
> ◆ All readers struggle with some kind of text.

These lessons help us collect information about our students. For example, when we teach a mini-lesson on expanding our definitions of reading, we look to see how students respond and how they define reading. When we teach a lesson on ways to record in a reading log, we look to see if students use new ideas quickly or stick with safe responses.

In the next section, we offer plans for mini-lessons that we typically teach in the first six weeks of school.

Mini-Lesson #1: Reading Is Thinking

Text Used: *Hippo! No, Rhino* by Jeff Newman (2006)

Goal of the Lesson: Students will begin to understand that reading is a thought process and learn to articulate that process. They will also come to understand that reading is more than getting the words right.

Why This Skill Is Important

Often our students come to us believing that reading is about getting the words right. We want to teach lessons that help these students redefine reading. We want them to talk together about the thinking that goes into reading. For this lesson, we choose books meant for very young children—books with very few words on a page, so students see how much thinking goes into reading any book, even those with few words.

Introducing the Lesson

"I have a new picture book today called *Hippo! No, Rhino* by Jeff Newman. This looks like a very easy book and I think you'll like it. But I am always so surprised at the amount of thinking that I

> **Books That Support Mini-Lessons on Thinking, Talking, and Writing About Reading**
>
> ◆ *The Essential 55* by Ron Clark
>
> ◆ *Marshfield Dreams* by Ralph Fletcher
>
> ◆ *Every Living Thing* by Cynthia Rylant
>
> ◆ *Guys Write for Guys Read* by Jon Scieszka
>
> ◆ *Knots in My Yo-Yo String* by Jerry Spinelli

do when I read, even with a book with very few words like this one. Today, while I'm reading, I'll stop at each page and give you time to pay attention to the things you are thinking about. You'll have time to write your thinking on sticky notes. Let's see how much thinking we do."

Reading the Book and Observing Students

After reading each page, Franki gives students time to mark their sticky notes, taking note of their writing behaviors, such as:

- Brandon wrote "I am not thinking anything."
- Shivani filled up all of her sticky notes during the first few pages.
- Hillary wrote one word on each sticky note.
- Jordan wrote connections on all his notes.

Engaging in Whole-Class Reflection

It is important that students process their thinking and begin to build a community definition of reading. During the whole-class reflection, we encourage this by asking these kinds of questions:

- How did it go?
- What did you notice?
- Was it hard or easy to pay attention to your own thinking?
- Did anyone notice that they were thinking mostly about predictions?
- Did anyone notice that they were thinking of something that was confusing?

What Are We Looking For?

- Is it natural for most students to attend to their thinking while reading?
- Are there a few students who need to be observed more closely?
- Do thoughts on a page all demonstrate the same kinds of thinking?

How Do We Plan Instruction Based on This Information?

Depending on what students write and how the whole-class reflection goes, we may devote more time to developing children's awareness of the thought process behind reading. If students are not yet comfortable talking and writing about their thinking, listening to other students sharing their thoughts on other simple picture books can help. Once they are comfortable talking and writing about their thinking, we can move on to lessons about different ways to think about reading different genres.

Jessica

I think some people took a feild trip to the zoo to see hippos

A sign says hippo and points to a Rhino so I think people will think the Rhino is a hippo

The Rhino wants the zookeeper's to change the sign. The Rhino is going crazy!

People are calling the Rhino a Hippo and the Rhino screams that the sign is not his.

Finally a person says that the Rhino is actually a Rhino.

The person changed the sign but for the hippo's sign it says porcupine-o.

Students used "talking bubble" sticky notes to track their thinking during the reading of a simple text. This lesson helped them redefine reading and begin to attend to their own thinking during reading.

Mini-Lesson #2: Supporting Opinions About Reading

Text Used: *Odd Jobs: The Wackiest Jobs You've Never Heard of* by Ellen Weiss (2000)

Goal of the Lesson: Students will learn to support their opinions with evidence from the text.

Why This Skill Is Important

We want students to be comfortable giving and supporting their opinions about a text, and using words directly from the text to give their opinions credibility. We usually do several lessons drawn from books, news magazines, the Internet, newspapers, and other sources. We always keep our eyes open for topics that our students will likely have an opinion about, such as wearing school uniforms, providing healthier school lunches, or changing the amount of homework. By using texts that invite different opinions, we help students think more deeply about a topic.

A book that we use early on is *Odd Jobs* by Ellen Weiss. In it, Weiss describes "roller coaster designer," "master sniffer," and other extremely odd jobs. Students are especially interested in this book. They enjoy discussing which jobs they would accept and which they would avoid and why. They naturally use the text to support their thinking on the topic.

Introducing the Lesson

Before the lesson, we choose a chapter from the book and then I introduce it to the whole class. "I want to share with you an excerpt from a book that I enjoy. The book is called *Odd Jobs*, and it is about interesting jobs that people have. Today we are going to read and discuss the section called 'Roller Coaster Designer.' I'll give you each copies of the text so that you can follow along. As I read, think about the things that you might want to talk about. What are your thoughts about this particular job?"

Reading the Book and Marking the Text

We then read the chapter aloud and give students time to mark the text by saying something like: "Before we get in small groups to talk about the text, I want to give you time to jot your thinking down. This might help you when you are in your groups. For the next few minutes, think about places in the text that might be interesting to talk about. You can use sticky notes or write directly on the copy of the text."

Observing Students in Small Groups

After a few minutes, we place students in groups of three or four to discuss the text. As we walk around, we listen for the ways students are bringing the text into the conversation. We write down things that students are saying so that we can share them with the rest of the class. Because we are thoughtful in our text selection, we usually have several students who bring the words from the text into the conversation. We might notice:

- Two students who disagree on an issue
- Students who marked text in effective ways
- A student who went back to read from the text to support his or her ideas

Engaging in Whole-Class Reflection

During the whole-class reflection, our role is to help students see the strategies and skills that will help them in book talks. So ask them these types of questions:

- How did it go?
- What did you notice?
- Did anyone use words, from the text when stating their opinion? How did using words from the text help you?
- Can anyone tell me about someone in the group who used the text to support his or her thinking? How did that help you understand what that person was saying?
- As you think back to the conversation, is there something in the text that you could have used to improve the conversation, but you forgot?

☺ **Ways to Build a Conversation**

- Connect to what other people say.
- Start a conversation that you think others will connect to.
- Say, "Let's talk about this some more."
- Notice what other people have marked.
- Start with something you've all marked.
- Say, "I thought that was interesting because..."
- Share things you know.
- Read the part you liked.
- Say, "I agree because..."
- Say, "I disagree because..."
- Ask questions about what people are saying.

This chart was created as part of a mini-lesson to help students learn ways to build a conversation.

What Are We Looking For?

- ◆ Is it natural for most students to use the text in the conversation?
- ◆ Are there a few students that I need to pull together in a small group for more practice?
- ◆ Did students notice when others were using the text?
- ◆ Do students seem to be using the text in effective ways?

How Do We Plan Instruction Based on This Information?

Depending on how the conversation and whole-class reflection goes, we may have to spend a few more days repeating the process. If using the text in conversations was hard for most students, we might do the same lesson several times. Or we may do similar lessons with different types of text. If there are only a few students who are struggling, we might pull them aside during independent reading, give them a different text, and help them mark it to build their skills in offering evidence-based opinions.

If students have difficulty building onto others' thoughts, we do a follow-up mini-lesson on having a productive conversation, and we continue to assess.

Mini-Lesson #3: Knowing Yourself as a Reader

For this lesson, we often use an excerpt from Anna Quindlen's *How Reading Changed My Life* (1998), a great book in which the author discusses her life as a reader. Many passages can be used to help students see the diversity of readers and to begin to see who they are as readers. For example, at one point, Quindlen talks about a favorite club chair that she used to sit in to read. This quote is a great way to start conversations about our favorite places to read. In essence, these conversations are lessons in thinking about one's own reading.

Mini-Lesson #4: Responding in Reading Logs

Some mini-lessons focus on the tools that we assign and how to get the most out of them. For example, one year, students were writing only simple connections in their reading logs. So Franki pulled some student samples from previous years to share with the class, and she and her students brainstormed all of the ways one could respond in a reading log. Students began to realize that many of the ways they responded in read-aloud would work for independent reading. The class created a chart as part of this mini-lesson to refer to when filling out reading logs.

During these weeks, Franki documents all of the interesting things that she notices about the readers in her classroom. Jotting things on sticky notes, adding to a child's profile sheet, or making a mental note helps Franki begin to put the information together.

> **Ways to respond in your Reading Log / Reading Notebook**
>
> - predictions
> - what's happening
> - use a line from the book
> - summarize
> - draw sketches
> - keep track of something that keeps coming up

A chart created as part of a mini-lesson to help students write more diverse log responses.

Small-Group Instruction

Because we want to make sure students are comfortable talking and thinking about themselves and their reading, we delay starting small-group meetings until after the routines are set and all of the students are comfortable with their strengths and weaknesses as readers. As students gain stamina over the first week or two of school, we spend that time having individual conferences. For the first six weeks, we use almost all of our time during independent reading to meet with students individually. We want students to know that this will be part of the daily routine and that talking about their reading with us and with classmates will be an important part of our reading workshop.

By avoiding small-group work at the beginning of the year, we send a message that we are not in charge of students' reading and that they are responsible for their independent reading. This gives them confidence and assurance that they are living their lives as readers. We want to start groups once we know our students well, we have our set routines, and students know themselves as readers well enough to have input.

Student-Initiated Groups

At the end of the first six weeks, we are ready to begin flexible, student-initiated groups in the reading workshop. This grouping often begins during the conversations we have with the whole class. When we know each child well and they know themselves well, it is easy to build a network in the classroom that can support student-initiated groups. We want to form our first groups by allowing students to tell *us* what they need. We ask them to share the challenges they are having and offer to form groups based on them. This way, students will understand that meeting in small groups is one way to meet their reading goals.

> ## Big Messages We Send During Small-Group Instruction
>
> - We can learn from one another.
> - Discussing our thinking with others helps us understand it better.
> - Lots of people in the class can help us reach our goals.
> - We can always find a group to support us.

Although we don't typically pull together many groups during the first six weeks, we do want students to get used to the idea of working in groups, as preparation for more consistent grouping later in the year. So during independent reading time, we post a sign-up sheet inviting students to participate in student-initiated groups on topics that might benefit them. For example, we may post a sign-up sheet for students who need help with choosing good books. Interested students sign up, and meet with that group for 15 to 20 minutes to help them choose books. Or we may notice that several students are unsure about reading aloud, so we offer a group on developing skills for reading aloud. Students who are interested in joining the group sign up, and we meet for a day or two during independent reading time to share some helpful strategies.

We are not prescriptive when forming these groups. We don't schedule a certain number of groups per day or require a certain amount of time per meeting. Instead, groups form and disband flexibly to help students identify ways they can grow as readers. If our goal is to plan instruction based on assessments, groups need to be flexible and fluid throughout the year. If we want students to reflect and set goals, groups can support them in their effort. Participating in a few student-initiated groups at the end of the first six weeks gets the students thinking about ways that groups can help them as they work toward their goals. As the year goes on, we initiate some groups. By then, students understand the purpose of small groups.

Once students have been engaged in student-initiated groups for a while, they become eager to suggest topics. One year, a student who wanted to talk about reading a particular series invited interested students to join a group on that topic. Another student may want to discuss a particular book she has been reading. And another may want to work on getting better at reading nonfiction. The possibilities for student-initiated groups are endless. We want students to understand that these groups are voluntary and that students are responsible for their own participation. When we provide the opportunity for student-initiated groups, students learn to reflect on their literacy and take responsibility for their learning.

Individual Reading Conferences and Share Time

At the beginning of the year, most of our time during independent reading is spent conferring with individual students, rather than working with small groups. Before we start any small-group work, we want to get to know our students individually and create clear profiles of them as readers. We want to collect information that will help us plan whole-group, small-group, and individual instruction. We want to give children the message that they are in charge of their reading during independent reading. Conducting conferences allows us to do all of these things.

Conferences are both informal and formal. We circulate around the room stopping by to chat casually with students about their reading and collect basic information about their level of engagement, book choice, and reading behaviors. We also conduct formal conferences during independent reading time—lengthier, more focused conferences. Students come to know that conferences will be a regular part of the reading workshop where we talk about books and who they are as readers.

> **Big Messages We Send During Individual Reading Conferences and Share Time**
>
> - We are interested in your history and preferences as a reader.
> - Talking and thinking about reading helps you reflect on your reading and set goals based on your reflections.
> - We are more interested in what you are doing as a reader than in what the book you are reading contains.
> - It helps others when you share things that you notice about your own reading.

Because we are honest about our work with students, we want them to be honest with us in return. We want them to know that we are a resource if they need it. We want students to understand our role during conference time. Our role is to do the following for our students:

- Learn about them as readers
- Support their growth as readers
- Discuss good books with them
- Think and talk together about their reading

At the end of reading workshop each day, the whole class participates in a five-minute share time that is important to our intellectual community. During these first six weeks of share, instead of talking about specific books, we focus on students' reading process by first asking, "What did you learn about yourself as a reader?" We learned this strategy from master teacher Sharon Taberski in her video series, *A Close-Up Look at Teaching Reading: Focusing on Children and Our Goals* (1995). This question can impact learning because it nudges students to think about their joys and struggles.

Share time is especially critical during the first few weeks of school. It gets the students to think about their processes as readers and pay attention to their own reading. Later in the year, the questions connect to what we notice about student reading during mini-lessons and conferring. But during the first six weeks, we repeat some of the same questions each day so students will know what to expect. We then add different questions based on what we observe in the reading workshop. We expand on Taberski's thinking by asking other process-related questions, which help students begin to put their thoughts about reading into words:

- Did reading go well today?
- How many of you stuck with a book that you started earlier this week? What made you stick with it? What made you want to quit?
- Did anyone feel like the time for reading was too long today?
- Will anyone choose a different spot to read tomorrow? Why was today's spot not good for you?
- Did anyone choose a book that wasn't right for you? How did you know it wasn't right?
- Did anyone get so lost in a book that you didn't hear anything? What did that feel like?
- Was anything going on in the room that bothered you? What can we do about that?

By spending the first six weeks addressing these questions during share time, we give students the language to think and talk about their reading for the rest of their lives. The questions we ask during share time serve two purposes: First, they teach the language students can begin to use on their own and with one another. Second, they give us valuable information about students and their reading processes, preferences, and habits.

As students respond to a question, we usually respond with a follow-up question. This helps students think past their initial ideas and gets them used to a technique that we use all year to raise the level of talk and reading. Students come to understand that for many questions, there are no "right" answers. We try to involve everyone in the conversation by asking a couple of nonthreatening questions. For example, if we ask, "Who had a good day in reading workshop?" students who are not comfortable speaking may be comfortable raising hands, or we may ask them to respond to a more demanding question with a partner, rather than with the whole class.

Share time provides another great opportunity to listen to what students are saying and to understand what they are learning. We can identify which children seem to be in tune with who they are as readers. We learn how students define reading by their comments. One year in Franki's class, Mei, a strong reader, mentioned that she was having trouble following the book that her sister had recommended. All students, those who are competent and those moving toward competency, often share what is hard for them. When struggling readers hear strong readers being honest about their challenges, they begin to realize that everyone is still learning to read.

Franki's Day-to-Day Record Keeping in the Reading Workshop

"For me, record keeping is a constantly evolving process. Strategies that seem to work well in some years don't seem to capture the essence of what I'm looking for in succeeding years."

—Timothy O'Keefe, *School Talk* (1997)

I recently attended a workshop where the presenter shared a great form for conferring. He also showed samples that told so much about the student. I left energized and was certain I had found the perfect conference form at last.

But, as you can probably guess, it was not the perfect form. It worked in some conferences but not in others. I continue to play with a record-keeping system that works for me, as most teachers do. Not only haven't I found the perfect conference form, I haven't found the perfect reading log or grouping sheet or any recording sheet for that matter. For our record-keeping system to inform our instruction, it should be ever changing. I have learned to be comfortable with the fact that no one form works for everything.

I have to remind myself often that there is a difference between record keeping and assessment. Just because I haven't written it down, doesn't mean that I haven't assessed a child. A comment could make a huge impact in my teaching, even if I don't document it. There are several reasons I keep records:

- To inform instruction
- To track progress
- To share with students
- To share with parents

The classroom is a busy place, and I don't have time to write down everything. So, I am constantly deciding what is worth writing down, what is worth keeping, and how best to make sense of my notes.

I have learned that my record-keeping system must match the goals I establish. I have to decide how I want to look at the information before I can determine the way to record it. So I ask myself:

- Am I focusing on one child?
- Do I want to discover patterns in the class? If so, what are they?
- Do I want to look at one specific strategy across the class? If so, what is it?

For example, when I want to look at the class as a whole—at patterns in the conferences for the week—I use the form below. But I also have forms for looking closely at individual students. There is not one form that meets all of my needs.

I also don't keep every note for the whole year. Many notes I take are on sticky notes or scrap paper. When the purpose of the note is, say, to remind myself of an observation to bring up in a conference, I only need the note until the conference. The forms that I use to show growth are a different story; they are stored in a binder as part of student records.

I believe that students can take responsibility for record keeping. Students keep their own logs, reflect on their work, collect samples, and so on. This is an important part of their lives as readers, and it helps them in setting goals and building an identity as a reader.

In this book, we share several record-keeping forms that Karen and I have used. Every form has worked at some point, for a specific purpose. We continue to search for that perfect record-keeping system, but we have found many that are almost perfect!

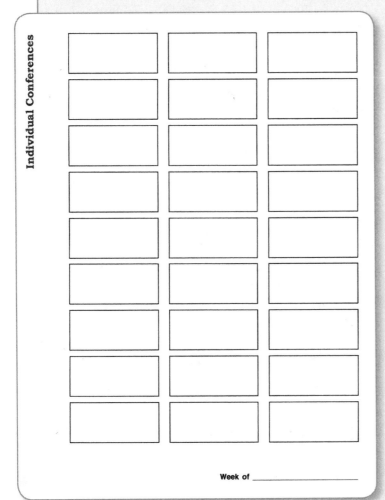

Individual Conferences

Week of _____

We use this form to document weekly conferences. It allows us to look at the class as a whole for any patterns to inform our instruction.

During the first six weeks, we try not to judge anything we hear during share time. If our goal is to get students noticing how they read, what they read, and who they are as readers, then we have to value what they notice. Early in the year, students often notice things that won't help them as readers. (For example, Franki's student Justin noticed that he always chose books with the letter "t" somewhere in the title.) We are trying to create an environment for students where it is safe to be honest about themselves as readers. We want to guide them to a higher level of awareness. Being nonjudgmental is critical to making that happen.

Status of the Class

Nancie Atwell introduced status of the class in her book *In the Middle: Writing, Reading, and Learning With Adolescents* (1987). Each day at the start of independent reading time, Nancie called out students' names. They responded by telling the title of the book they were reading and the page they were on. We started this same routine years ago when we first implemented a reading workshop, and we are still practicing it today. The quick check-in is, in essence, a short conference with each child. It provides great information and starts lots of conversations that we can build on. Taking the status of the class each day is a way to do the following:

- Document each child's reading
- Allow students to hear what other children are reading
- See how each child is progressing through a book
- Model questions for students and new ways to think about their reading
- Monitor how quickly students are finishing books
- Track the variety of genres students are reading

Franki asks questions of a few students each day as she calls their names. For example, when Mia started a new book, Franki asked how she heard about it. When Riley started a book before she completed another, Franki asked why she decided to switch books. Other questions Franki may ask when students respond to the status of the class include the following:

- Is that a new author for you?
- Have you read any other books in that series?
- Who recommended the book to you?

We also use the status of the class to connect students with other readers who have similar tastes. When Sonia started *Amber Brown* (Danziger, 1994), Franki suggested she talk to Jessica, who had read several in the series. When Kylie wanted to quit *The City of Ember* (DuPrau, 2005), Franki suggested that she talk to Brennen, who had finished the book, because he could help her get through a tough part. Conversation during status of the class is natural and quick, but it sets the stage for much deeper conversations and provides a way to collect important information about the reading lives of our students.

We used to worry that calling out names and listening for book titles distracts students as they settle into their books. We now believe that the benefits outweigh the cost because students get a sense of what the class is reading and they listen for books they may be interested in later. When students hear Franki's questions, they begin to think in new ways about their reading.

The status-of-the-class form to the right shows a typical range of student responses. Franki uses codes to help the process go quickly (Q=quit book, F=finished book). She may also write quick notes about what students are doing (rereading with sticky notes, starting their fourth Judy Moody book).

Name	Hannah		
Date	Title	Page	
10-10	Aquamarine	26	Q
10-12	Babymouse Rockstar	8	F
10-13	Arthur's Teeth	1	
10-16	Fairy Dust... Egg	1	Q
10-17	Judy Moody	26	
10-18	Judy Moody	38	
10-19	Judy Moody	112	F
10-23	Charlotte's Web	26	
10-24	"	32	
10-25	"	47	
10-26	"	57	
10-30	"	148	
11-1	"	159	
11-6	Spiderwick Field Guide		
11-7	Judy Moody Gets Famous	24	
11-8	"	76	
11-9	"	87	
11-10	Judy Moody Predicts the Future	1	
11-13	"	48	
11-14	"	79	
11-15	"	119	
11-16	Amelia's Best Year Ever	1	
11-17	Ugly Princess	22	Q
11-20	Ivy + Bean #1	1	
11-21	Ivy + Bean	16	
11-27	Ivy + Bean	72	

We fill out the status-of-the-class form several days a week to track students' reading. This allows us to look at a child's reading over time.

Reading Interviews

Our first more formal reading conference is the reading interview. Typically, we interview every child in the class using the same questions and taking notes. We might notice that a particular book series is popular or that many students find poetry boring. Or we may notice that many students don't have a favorite author, but they do have friends who recommend books to them. We pay attention to patterns across the class, as well as information about individual students. The information we gather during reading interviews, along with all the other data we have collected, helps us plan thoughtful instruction for our students. In interviews, we might ask questions like these:

- How would you describe yourself as a reader?
- What are you currently reading?
- What are you going to read next?
- How do you choose the books you read?
- What kind of reading is easy for you?
- What kind of reading is hard for you?

Name _Justin_ Date _8/31_

How would you describe yourself as a reader?
like fantasy
like Magic Treehouse

What are you currently reading?
The City of Ember
Magic Treehouse – "I've read 10"

What kinds of things did you read over the summer?
I don't really think I read this summer.

What kinds of things do you like to read?
things about animals

What kinds of things do you NOT like to read?
biographies
Amber Brown – "not my kind of book"

Do you read any magazines or newspapers?
MAD Magazine

Is there a series that you like to read? Why?
Magic Treehouse 'don't know

Do you have a favorite author?
No

Do you have a favorite book?
Magic Treehouse

What are you going to read next?
City of Ember – "my limit – it's a huge book"

How do you choose the books you read?
title

[sticky note:] enjoys fantasy
check engage-
ment
no summer
rdg.
previewing → teach

Do you talk to anyone about the books you read? Who?
not really

What do the other people in your family read?
DaVinci Code

What kinds of books do your friends read?
I don't know

What do you do when you get stuck?
sound it out

What do you do when you start to read each day?
turn to the page I left off

How do you keep track of the characters in the books you are reading?
"it's easy"

What kind of reading is easy for you?
Magic Treehouse

What kind of reading is hard for you?
fat books

What are you most proud of in your reading?
I'm good at it.

A copy of the reading interview adapted from *Still Learning to Read* (Sibberson & Szymusiak, 2003). This interview is given orally early in the year. We take notes but use the interview questions to start yearlong conversations. The attached sticky note reminds us of things that we noticed during the interview.

We believe strongly that students should live authentic lives as readers in our classrooms. Following each interview, we want to put the information together for ourselves. We start by asking ourselves questions that help us focus on our main goals during the first six weeks—helping all students see themselves as readers. By thinking about the patterns of answers to the interview, we can add to each child's profile.

Questions	Implications
Does the student know himself as a reader?	Help students learn to reflect and recognize their strengths, challenges, and interests.
Does the student have favorite authors?	Help students begin to develop preferences as a reader.
What kind of texts do they read?	Identify students who read/do not read a variety of books.
What do they do when they get stuck?	Build on strategies that students have to make sense of texts that are difficult.
How do students choose the books they read?	Identify students who need help and support to choose books.

Student Goal Setting

Throughout the first six weeks, we are trying to help our students know themselves as readers. Goal setting becomes worthwhile once students have that knowledge. We begin goal setting early in the year. We want our students to feel comfortable talking about their strengths and challenges as readers. We want them to understand that we are all different as readers and that readers have goals. Goal setting allows every child to move forward as a reader. No matter what kind of readers they are, goal setting helps them see that there is always something to celebrate and something to work on. Students often set goals about the kinds of books they will read, the amount of time they will read, and the strategies they will use to deepen their understanding. We know that early in the year, our students' goals may be very shallow or go against everything we believe about reading. For example, Kelly told Franki that she wanted to read fatter books. This is not a goal we have for students, but it tells us so much about what Kelly thinks about reading. It is hard to keep quiet when students respond in this way. We often feel like we should intervene and tell them that fatter does not necessarily mean better, but if our goal is to help children believe that they are in charge of their learning, we have to value where they are, knowing that during the year, their goals will become more realistic.

In *Shades of Meaning: Comprehension and Interpretation in Middle School*, Donna Santman discusses the need to ask students specific questions. "Instead of asking questions about their general lives, I decided to start in a more sensitive place by asking the kids first and foremost, 'When do you fake read and why? That is, when do you act as if you are reading and you really aren't?'" (2005, p. 23) Santman knows that some questions give us good information about our students, especially specific questions that invite students to be honest with us about their lives as readers. Santman allows her students to talk honestly about a part of their reading lives that they weren't sure was acceptable.

So, as students share during whole-class reflection, our questions become more specific:

- Did anybody quit a book this week?
- Did anybody find a new author they liked?
- Did anybody catch themselves fake reading this week?
- Did anybody start their reading and forget where they were in the story?
- Did anybody find a place in their book where it was hard to get a picture in their head?

These questions help students notice aspects of their reading they may not have thought about before. The answers, in turn, give them options for goal setting. Some common weekly goals during the first several weeks of school include:

- Finish the book I am reading
- Read more pages each day
- Stick with one book

Pulling All the Assessments Together

For six weeks we collect information about each child and about the class as a whole, through formal and informal assessments. By the time we hold parent conferences in October, we can pull together all that information. We are able to look at patterns to think about goals and next steps for each child. Parent conferences in our district take place two times each year— once in the fall and once in the spring.

Franki recently started to share the student profile with parents during conferences. The assessment web captures everything we know about a student's literacy development. (See page 60 for an example.) In addition to reading, it provides a look at all areas of literacy, including notes from independent reading, read-aloud, and individual reading interviews, notes from formal assessments as well as some district writing and spelling assessments. Franki includes information on norm-referenced standardized tests from the previous year so they can see whether assessments are saying the same thing or not.

Formal Assessments During the First Six Weeks

The Developmental Reading Assessment (DRA) is a performance assessment that is administered to students individually. In our school district we administer the DRA to all K to 8 students during the first six weeks of school. We consider it a very valuable tool in our assessment process.

We usually don't administer the DRA until after student interviews have been completed and numerous informal conferences are well underway. Starting the year with the DRA would send the wrong message. At the beginning of the year, we want students to know that we are interested in their reading lives. We want our first conference to be more informal than the DRA. We want them to know that we are eager to find out about what they read. We don't want to confuse that message with an assessment that relies on oral reading and comprehension questions too early. By giving the DRA later in the fall, we can send a message that we believe there are many ways to learn about our students as readers and we can learn from them in formal and informal ways.

We begin the assessment by asking students to complete

Teacher Observation Guide	**All the Way Under**			Level 40, Page 6
Engagement	Intervention	Instructional	Independent	Advanced
Wide Reading	1 General reading materials (*e.g.*, chapter books, comics)	2 Titles generally below-grade-level; limited reading experiences	3 Some titles within 2–3 genres or multiple books within a genre; generally on-grade-level texts	4 Wide variety of titles across 3 or more genres; many on- and above-grade-level texts
Self-Assessment and Goal-Setting	1 Vague or no strength and/or goal; may not be directly related to reading	2 Vague strength(s) and goal(s) identified; vague or no plan	3 Strengths and goals related to the reading process/behaviors; relevant plan	4 Multiple strengths and specific goals related to the reading process/behaviors; multiple-step plan
Score	2 3	4 5	6 7	8
Oral Reading Fluency				
Expression	1 Little expression; monotone	2 Some expression that conveys meaning	3 Expression reflects mood, pace, and tension at times	4 Expression reflects mood, pace, and tension most of the time
Phrasing	1 Short phrases	2 Longer word phrases some of the time	3 Longer, meaningful phrases most of the time	4 Consistently longer, meaningful phrases
Rate	1 Slow with long pauses and repetitions	2 Moderate with some pauses and repetitions	3 Adequate with a few pauses and/or repetitions	4 Very good
Accuracy Rate	1 90–94%	2 95–96%	3 97–98%	4 99–100%
Score	4 5 6	7 8 9 10	11 12 13 14	15 16
Comprehension Skills/Strategies				
Prediction	1 Illogical or unrelated prediction and/or question	2 1 or 2 reasonable predictions and/or questions related to the text	3 Several reasonable predictions and questions related to the text	4 Several thoughtful predictions and questions directly related to the text
Summary	1 1–2 events in own language and/or copied text; may include incorrect information	2 Partial summary; generally in own language; some important characters/ events; may include misinterpretation	3 Adequate summary in own language; important characters' names, many of the important events, some details/vocabulary	4 Adept summary in own language; important characters' names, most important events, details/vocabulary
Literal Comprehension	1 Little information from the text and/or included incorrect information	2 Some information from the text; may include misinterpretation	3 Included information from the text that accurately responds to question(s) or prompt(s)	4 Important information from the text effectively responds to question(s) or prompt(s)
Interpretation	1 Little or no understanding of important text implications	2 Some understanding of important text implications; little or no details	3 Understands important text implications; relevant supporting details	4 Insightful understanding of important text implications; important supporting details
Reflection	1 Insignificant or unrelated message or event	2 Vaguely related or less significant message or event; general or no statement(s) to support opinion	3 Important message or event; relevant statement(s) to support opinion	4 Significant message (beyond the literal level or event; insightful statement(s) to support opinion
Metacognitive Awareness	1 Vague explanation of the use of 1 strategy or unrelated response	2 Brief explanation of the use of 1 or more strategies; vague or general statement(s)	3 Adequate explanation of the use of 1 or more strategies; specific examples from the text	4 Effective explanations of the use of more than 1 strategy; explicit examples from the text
Score	6 7 8 9 10	11 12 13 14 15 16	17 18 19 20 21 22	23 24

Add the circled numbers in each section together to obtain scores for reading engagement, oral reading fluency, and comprehension skills/strategies.

10

DRA™ Grades 4–6 © Pearson Education, Inc./Celebration Press/Pearson Learning Group. All rights reserved.

a brief survey about their reading. We learn about their favorite books and authors, as well as goals they have as readers. The survey identifies students' reading behaviors, which can help us determine how we can move them toward independence.

In the next part of the DRA, the student reads a small portion of an appropriate text aloud while the teacher completes a running record to determine a level of accuracy. The teacher can also determine the level of fluency in the student's oral reading. The student is then asked to make predictions about the rest of the text. The student continues to read the book independently and answers questions about the text to determine his or her level of comprehension. It is helpful to know how deeply the student understands what he has read.

The DRA is a valuable tool because it gives us a look at the student's response to the survey and helps to determine his or her level of accuracy, fluency, and comprehension. It measures reading achievement, monitors growth over time, and provides critical information for planning instruction for the class and individual students.

The DRA scoring sheets help us document information about individual students and also recognize patterns in the class. After reviewing the results of the DRA, we can begin to plan whole-class lessons that meet the needs of many students. We can also plan how we will move forward with small-group instruction and reading conferences.

We learn a great deal from the DRA that we can use in future instructional planning, such as who needs support in fluency and who is struggling with comprehension. We believe that the DRA provides a great tool for learning about the students' reading behaviors. It gives us a student's level of accuracy in reading, and allows us to understand many other things about the child as a reader, such as whether he or she looks at an entire unknown word to solve it or whether he or she only uses the first letter. The DRA helps us think about strategic reading and fluency. All of this information helps us plan for student learning. It helps us focus on the explicit learning that each child needs and helps us design learning experiences that will promote more independent reading.

An assessment web, shared with parents at conferences, compiles much of the assessment information that we have gathered about a student during the first six weeks of school.

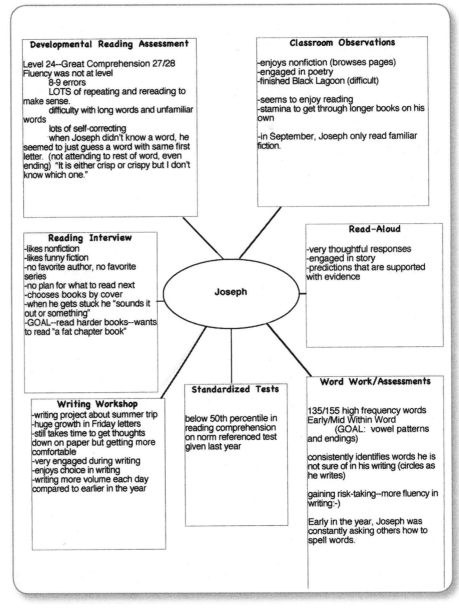

Developmental Reading Assessment

Level 24--Great Comprehension 27/28
Fluency was not at level
    8-9 errors
    LOTS of repeating and rereading to make sense.
    difficulty with long words and unfamiliar words
    lots of self-correcting
    when Joseph didn't know a word, he seemed to just guess a word with same first letter. (not attending to rest of word, even ending) "It is either crisp or crispy but I don't know which one."

Classroom Observations

-enjoys nonfiction (browses pages)
-engaged in poetry
-finished Black Lagoon (difficult)

-seems to enjoy reading
-stamina to get through longer books on his own

-in September, Joseph only read familiar fiction.

Reading Interview
-likes nonfiction
-likes funny fiction
-no favorite author, no favorite series
-no plan for what to read next
-chooses books by cover
-when he gets stuck he "sounds it out or something"
-GOAL--read harder books--wants to read "a fat chapter book"

Read-Aloud

-very thoughtful responses
-engaged in story
-predictions that are supported with evidence

Joseph

Writing Workshop
-writing project about summer trip
-huge growth in Friday letters
-still takes time to get thoughts down on paper but getting more comfortable
-very engaged during writing
-enjoys choice in writing
-writing more volume each day compared to earlier in the year

Standardized Tests

below 50th percentile in reading comprehension on norm referenced test given last year

Word Work/Assessments

135/155 high frequency words
Early/Mid Within Word
    (GOAL: vowel patterns and endings)

consistently identifies words he is not sure of in his writing (circles as he writes)

gaining risk-taking--more fluency in writing:-)

Early in the year, Joseph was constantly asking others how to spell words.

The assessment information must provide a complete profile of each child as a reader and learner. We cannot look at any one area without taking into account all we have learned about a student. To do that, we need to look at the webs with the following questions in mind:

- What are the child's strengths?
- When is the child most engaged during the day?
- How does he see himself as a reader?
- What jumps out as a big goal for the child?
- Are there obvious patterns to her learning?
- Are the assessments consistent or do they tell us different things?
- How does the child's attitude about reading relate to performance?
- Do formal and informal assessments show the same things?

Once we have gathered answers to these questions, we ask ourselves the most important questions:

- What one or two goals are most critical for this child right now?
- What's next?

As we pull our assessment information together for parent conferences, we realize just how much we know about each student. We are prepared to move our students to independence because we know their strengths and challenges. We can plan thoughtfully and purposefully and create individualized learning experiences for our students. We can gradually release responsibility for learning to our students as they become more sophisticated. It is a hopeful time.

Concluding Thoughts

In the remainder of the book, we look at the routines we initiate during the first six weeks in greater depth. We share how we continue to gather critical information about our students during each routine. We discuss our assessments and how they become more seamless as we move through the year, and our expectations for students and how they change throughout the year. We also discuss new information we can gain about our students.

Chapter 3

Independent Reading

One day Maggie asked Franki if she could go to the library to see if they had the first book in the Bailey School Kids series. Franki told her that she could, but reminded her that there were about 20 different Bailey School Kids books in a basket in the classroom library. Maggie was adamant, though. She wanted the *first* book in the series. She hadn't read any books in the series yet and she *always* reads the first book first. Franki told her that this series was written so that you didn't have to read them in order, and Maggie said, "I decided to always read books in order. Last year, I started the Harry Potter series with the second book. There were all of these characters that I didn't know and I was confused, so now I always read series books in order."

During independent reading time our students discover who they are as readers. Although it is tempting to control their reading, as Franki tried with Maggie, we know that independent reading time is most effective if students are in control. We can direct them to a certain section of the classroom library or require them to select the books we know they can read at an independent level, but this doesn't really help them in the long run. Maggie and the other students in Franki's classroom are in control of their independent reading. They can decide, for example, whether they are the kind of reader who likes to read series books in order or the kind who goes through phases of reading books by one great author. They are confident about who they are as readers and know that Franki is there to support them.

Independent reading is key. Without ample time, students don't really own their reading. The reading workshop becomes stale and teacher directed. That's why independent reading takes up the biggest block of our reading workshop time (30 to 45 minutes each day). During this time, we meet with students in individual conferences and in small groups as other students read on their own. Students see independent reading time as an important and enjoyable part of their school day, a time when they can try out new strategies, come to understand the kinds of readers they are, and take charge of their own reading lives.

We want more than anything for students to be successful when they are reading independently. Our work in mini-lessons, read-aloud, share time, conferences, and small-group instruction empowers students to read and understand text independently and to build strategies they can use throughout their lives. All of our routines provide students with the tools they need to read and understand a variety of texts. Independent reading is no exception.

Choosing Texts for Independent Reading

For a long time, we wanted our students to read chapter books during independent reading time because it seemed to help them build stamina for reading books from cover to cover. We broadened our perspective when we read David Booth's *Reading Doesn't Matter Anymore: Shattering the Myths of Literacy* (2006), in which he reminds us, "A future literate culture will be determined not only by its literature—fiction or non-fiction—but also by newspapers, magazines, television, computers, networks, films, CD-Roms, hypertext, e-mail, and other forms yet to be created" (p. 27). If our goal is to support lifelong, independent reading, we cannot allow students to read only novels. The key is placing value on *all* genres and types of reading materials so that students experience the variety they will encounter outside of school.

If our students are just sitting quietly with books, we know that they aren't growing as readers. Offering a variety of texts prevents that from happening. We ask students to choose texts they can read from front to back. If they choose a newspaper, magazine, or a nonfiction book, we ask them to find a portion of text they will read from beginning to end.

Independent reading time provides a great opportunity for assessment. We spend most of the time meeting with students in small groups and individually, but we also devote plenty of time to observing. When we make ourselves available during independent reading time, we learn more about students as readers because they are more likely to come to us for informal chats. They are more likely to share something in their reading, ask a quick question or invite us into a conversation about their reading. It's important that we leave time each day to just "hang out," observe, and interact with our students when called upon to do so.

Reading Nonfiction and Poetry

Observing students during independent reading can help us make decisions about expanding the opportunities we give them. For example, Franki recently realized that students were excited about reading fiction—so much, in fact, that they didn't want to read nonfiction or poetry. The students were reading nonfiction within content areas, but Franki wanted them to find the same joy in nonfiction and poetry during independent reading. So she began two new morning routines: nonfiction reading time and Poetry Friday! On nonfiction reading days, students arrive at school each morning and settle in with nonfiction reading material that they choose. They discover all kinds of texts that they had never thought of reading before, such as *Dogs and Cats* (Jenkins, 2007), *What Stinks?* (Singer, 2006), and *Satchel Paige* (Cline-Ransome, 2003). Poetry Friday! is a wonderful, literacy-rich way to begin the day and end the week. Each Friday, students gather around the room to read poetry and enjoy doughnuts and juice together for 15 minutes. At the end of this time, some students share poems they've enjoyed.

After several weeks of carrying out these routines, more poetry and nonfiction started to surface during independent reading time. Franki found that by dedicating a bit of time to these two types of reading, she gave students the opportunity to discover genres that they had come to love.

Supporting Independence With Classroom Libraries

Learning to choose appropriate books is essential to independent reading, so we try to set up our classroom libraries to support that. Many of our books are organized into baskets by authors, series, and genres that students enjoy. We also gather fiction, nonfiction, and poetry into distinct sections of the classroom to make books in those genres easy to find and browse, and encourage students to think about their purpose for reading when choosing a book.

Fiction

The fiction section contains chapter books, novels, picture books, and graphic novels organized in baskets by author and/or series. We want students to realize that if they like a book by a certain author, they might like other books by the same author. If students feel comfortable reading a particular book in a series, they can go back to the basket for another book in that series. Instead of focusing on reading levels, we place value on choosing books based on authors, series, or characters students enjoy.

Nonfiction

The nonfiction books are organized in baskets by topic, such as dinosaurs, United States history, or interesting people. Some baskets hold books by particular nonfiction authors, such as Seymour Simon, Gail Gibbons, and April Pulley Sayre. Others hold series books such as the DK Eyewitness books. According to Christine Duthie, author

Fiction is organized into baskets by author and series.

of *True Stories: Nonfiction Literacy in the Primary Classroom,* "Arranging books by topic within genres gives individual nonfiction titles added power: four books on a single topic grouped together on the same shelf seem to gain significance. For example, an older book about caring for a pet has less appeal when it is randomly mixed in with fiction and other nonfiction than when it is one title among a larger collection of books on pets. A child committed to a certain topic is more apt to read all the available books on that topic if they are housed side by side" (1996, p. 12). This is true in our experience because reading one book on a topic often invites new questions about it.

Poetry

Books in this section are organized in an area of the room on a shelf of their own. Most books face spine out, but throughout the year, we may highlight books by certain poets or books that are fun to read aloud by displaying them in the poetry section.

In addition to the three major sections we describe above, a few areas contain picture books and novels that are stored spine out for browsing, which is a great way to find surprises.

We rotate books and baskets in all areas of the library as we learn about our students as readers. After many years of teaching, we have found that the tastes and skills of every class evolve. So, as we learn about students as readers, we may put away some books and add others. Last year, Franki's class fell in love with two series—Babymouse by Jennifer and Matt Holm and Ivy and Bean by Annie Barrows. Since it was important to her students, Franki added two new baskets for these two beloved series. At another point in the year, several of Franki's students were stuck on Matt Christopher books because they loved to read about sports. She wanted them to expand their choices a bit, so she created a basket of other sports-related fiction books as an invitation to these readers.

Nonfiction is organized into baskets by topic.

The organization of our library also supports our work in conferences. Often, when we discover that a student needs support in choosing good books, we hold our conference in the library section that we feel may appeal to the student, or we carry a few of the baskets to a table to preview together. By arranging the books in baskets, we help students choose the next book they will read as well as suggest books they might enjoy reading down the line.

Learning About New Books

If we are going to guide students in making wise choices, we need to stay current on new books. We spend a great deal of time reading book reviews, browsing catalogs and Web sites, and talking to others in the know. We certainly don't feel like we have to read every book in our library, but we do have to be familiar with them all. So we try to keep up with new books, expand our expertise to include a larger variety of texts, and recall old favorites that our students might enjoy. As we listen to students throughout the day, we think about new books that might stretch them. We want to help them develop tastes and preferences. We use what we know about each child to help him or her choose engaging books.

One year, upon finishing a book, Haylie conferred with Franki about choosing her next book. Once Franki realized this pattern, she decided to help Haylie to "think ahead" in her reading. Each year, Franki introduces next-read bags or boxes, so students can gather several texts they might want to read in the future. Franki spent a conference session helping Haylie preview books from several series, and encouraged her to create her own next-read box. As a result, Haylie discovered that she liked the Katie Kazzo series and, in turn, was more engaged during independent reading.

Maggie was equally dependent on Franki for book advice. Franki realized that she had tastes similar to those of a few other girls in the room. Since Maggie was very social, having a network of friends to recommend books to her could help her become more independent. Franki asked a few of the girls to share some of their favorite books with Maggie. The group chatted for an entire independent reading time, and Maggie left with book ideas to last her a while. Not only did she find good books, she built relationships with other readers who could recommend books in the future.

Students keep books that they may want to read in the future in next-read bags or boxes.

Students help one another find books for their next-read boxes.

Assessing During Independent Reading

Independent reading time offers so many opportunities to assess student progress. Here are some of the things we do:

- Analyze reading logs to learn about students' reading patterns. We also encourage students to reflect on their logs to discover what they can learn about themselves as readers.

- Take the status of the class each day to become familiar with what students are doing and decide how and when to support them in their reading.

- Learn from the students' reflections about their own reading and the reading goals they identify for themselves.

- Listen to conversations and observe students during independent reading time.

Each of these methods allows us to learn more about our students as readers and to think about the support they need to become more independent.

Traditional Reading Logs

We require students to record their reading in a log for the entire year. Typically, we ask students to write the book title, author, the pages they read in each session, and reflections they have about their reading. The log provides a handy record of a child's reading. We can glance at it to see the variety of books a child is reading, how long it takes her to finish books, and other important trends. At several points in the year, we take a hard look at each child's log, thinking about what instruction is needed. We also think about the patterns we see in the class and determine what kind of whole-class lessons might be of benefit.

Encouraging Self-Reflection

It is important for students to see their readings logs as powerful tools for yearlong reflection. We ask students to look over their logs and share anything that they notice. This helps us to know how skilled they are at reflecting on their own reading. If their reflection is shallow, we can help them develop strategies

---

Questions We Ask Ourselves When Looking at a Child's Reading Log

- Is this child reading a variety of genres?
- Does this child seem to have a favorite author or genre?
- Is this child finishing most books in a week or two? Or is he or she reading the same book for long periods of time?
- Is this child reading the same books at home and at school or is he or she reading two different books? Is this system working for the child?
- Is this child consistent in the amount that he or she reads daily?
- Is this child stuck in a genre?
- Has this child quit a lot of books?

Questions to Help Students Reflect on Reading Logs

- Is there a genre or author that you have enjoyed more than others lately?
- Are you reading a variety of books or are you hooked on one author or series?
- Do you see any type of book that is missing from your reading?
- Are you reading the same book at home and at school? How is that working?
- What do you notice about the number of books you are finishing?
- Do you notice any patterns in your book selection—maybe you read a long book, then a short book? Or maybe you read a series for a few books and then move to something else?
- Have you quit any books? Was that a good decision? Why or why not?
- Are there any books that you have read faster or slower than other books? Why do you think that happened?

for deeper thinking. Earlier in the year, we spend a bit more time asking questions that encourage students to reflect, but after some time they are better able to reflect without any prompting.

With answers to these questions, we can determine where our teaching should go. For example, if students admit that quitting lots of books is a problem for them, we need to pull them together in a group to work on building stamina or choosing better books. Some students will realize that after reading a challenging book, they return to a more comfortable book. We keep that in mind in case that strategy could help other readers. Over time, students begin to take responsibility for the things they notice. Instead of our telling students that they need more variety in their reading, they can see it clearly when we ask them to articulate their reflections. Students often end up setting goals for themselves that we would have set, but they are more dedicated to meeting those goals because they set them.

Name Sruti T.

Date	Title	Page
10-10-06	The theif lord	7 PS.
10-12-06	The Theif lord	3 PS
10-13-06	Junie b jones Yucky blucky frutcake	15 ½ PS
10-14-06	The Theif Lord	10 PS
10-15-06	The theif Lord	5 PS
10-19-06	The theif Lord	3 PS
10-20-06	Junie B. Yucky Blucky ...	17 PS
10-22-06	Junie B Monkey Buisness	10 PS
10-23-06	Junie B Monkey Buisness	10 PS
10-24-06	There was Somthing big here	2 PS
10-25-06	Junie B. Monkey	20 PS
10-26-06	Junie B. Monkey	10 PS
10-22-06	Junie b monkey	23 PS
10-28-06	Lizzie for President	10 PS
10-29-06	Lizzie for President	21 PS
11-1-06	Buissness week	Finished
11-3-06	Mr. Brown can moo can you?	Finished
11-4-06	Go dog go!	Finished
11-5-06	Red fish Bluefish yellow fish...	Finished
11-7-06	Junie b Jones Aloha-ha-ha	Finished
11-10-06	Junie b Jones is a party animal	16 PS
11-12-06	Junie b Jones is a party animal	17 PS
11-15-06	Junie b jones is a party animal	20 PS
11-18-06	There is a wocket in my...	Finished
11-20-06	Natures art box & Junie b Jingle	Finished / 10 PS

Students record daily reading in their reading logs. We use the logs to help us think about students' independent reading. On this form, we notice that Sruti is finishing books and is bouncing between easy picture books and difficult chapter books. She spent a great deal of time reading Junie B. Jones and completing the books in the series that she started.

Reflection and Goal-Setting Forms

Periodically, we encourage students to write about what they notice in their logs. This gives the child an opportunity to really look at her reading and set reading goals. It also saves us time. While we certainly look at individual logs, it is often faster and easier to pick out patterns and plan instruction by flipping through a stack of reflection forms. The reflection forms also become springboards for individual conferences. Since students have already thought about their reading, they are ready to talk about what they have discovered. They are also ready to think more deeply about their needs as readers.

Name _Conner_   Date _3|21_

Use your reading log to answer the following questions.

When looking at your log, what do you notice about your reading?
I read lots of sports books and read at lest 10 pages each day.

Are you reading a variety of books or are you stuck in a genre?
I did read all sports and I jumped out if it.

Do you have some idea of books that you want to read after you finish your current book? Which books might you read?
I am going to read the spider wick sereys.

How do you choose books? What are some ways that you decide which book to read next?
I take a book that I would read or read a book that I have herd of.

Which books have you quit? Was that a good decision? Why or why not?
I have not quit a book and I think I don't need to because I like the book I choughs

Do you have anything that you want to work on in the ways you choose books?
Read the Spider wick Sereys because I want to see vore there go on intvenchers.

Students reflect on their reading logs at several points during the year.

Name Sydney   Date 10-26

Reading Log—1ˢᵗ Quarter Reflection

List the books that you finished this quarter (home and school)

saddle club, Horse in the house, Fox in the frost, amelias family ties, luv amelia luv nadia,

List any books that you read part of—or that you quit before you were finished.

So little time, Chicken Soup for the kids soul, Animal Ark, lab in the lawn,

Did you find any new authors/series that you like?

chicken Soup, Amelia books

List all of the different genres that you've read.

Fiction, nonfiction, mystery,

Is there a book that you'd like to read next quarter?

the Volcano disaster, chasing vermer, the tal of Despereaux, Chicken soup for the horse lover soul, Holes.

What are you most proud of in your reading this quarter?

finishing So many books and trying a new Series

What is a goal that you have for next quarter?

reading more pages at one reding half hour

Self-Created Reading Logs

Although a traditional log works fine for most classes, that's not always the case. For example, one year Franki's students started out with a traditional log, but after the first few months, the students did not see the value in them. They saw the log as something to fill out, as an assignment. They were merely going through the motions.

So Franki thought long and hard about the real purposes of logs. During a visit to a bookstore, she noticed a variety of published logs designed to support specific activities—bird-watchers' logs, runners' logs, dieters' logs, and others. She realized that logs were important in many areas of life. She remembered keeping diet logs and exercise logs at various times in her life. These logs helped her meet specific goals.

At the time, Franki was teaching at the same school as Sharon Hathaway, a physical education teacher and marathon runner. The students were well aware of all of the races Sharon ran. Franki asked Sharon if she kept logs and, of course, she did. Sharon came into the classroom and shared several of her logs with Franki's class. Her reasons for keeping logs included:

- Tracking her weekly mileage
- Recording when she starts with a new pair of running shoes
- Reflecting on reasons she had a good running day
- Reflecting on reasons she had a bad running day
- Watching for injuries
- Tracking days off
- Staying focused on her plan
- Setting goals
- Recording total mileage for the year
- Comparing races by looking back
- Giving her confidence right before a race to see what she's accomplished
- Planning her race training

Sharon showed the students how she sets goals. She talked about how she depended on her log to reflect on things like whether the foods she ate influenced her running. She designed each log specifically for the goal that she was trying to accomplish, so no two were the same. The log design depended on the race she was running and the goals she set for herself.

Following Sharon's visit, Franki invited the students to create their own reading logs. She advised them to think about their goals as readers, based on the first several months of school, and design a log that would help them track their progress. Most students were excited. During independent reading time for the next day or two, many students were very thoughtful about their logs. Some students chose to stay with the traditional reading log. Many used the traditional log as a template, but added sections to meet their goals.

Others revamped the log entirely to address very specific challenges they were facing. For example, one student realized that she was not making thoughtful predictions in her independent reading. So she created a place for daily predictions, hoping it would help her develop this habit. For another student, staying engaged in reading for the entire 30 to 45 minutes was a challenge. So each time she looked up at the clock during independent reading, she would make a tally mark in her self-created log. By paying attention to this habit, she could track how much time she was actually reading each day. These self-created logs helped students realize the power of reflecting and goal setting in their reading.

		Pages
Monday Date=Oct.29,2004	Predictions I don't think the dad will go away. Will the mom and dad stay enimeis? Why did the author put in fighting? Why does Joey want to see his parents fight. Why did the mom say "oh my gosh" when they were fighting? What would Joey do?	8–14
Tuesday Date=Nov.30,2004	Predictions I think the dad will die? Why did the dad sneak out of the hospital? Who's Booth? What Would Joey Do?	16–31
Wedensday Date=Dec1,2004	Predictions I think the gnomes will come up again. Why does the dad talk about getting married?	31–48
Thursday Date=Dec.2,2004	Predictions Why did the dad come back? Why doesn't the mom care about Joey? What Would Joey D?	82–96
Friday Date=Dec.3,2004	Predictions I think that Olivia and Joey will be friends. Pages 96–112	Goal ■ Finish my book (What would Joey Do?)

name Rebecca   week of ___

	Mon.	Tue.	Wed.	Thu.	Fri.
Title	Ruby Holler	Ruby Holler	Ruby Holler	Ruby Holler	Ruby Holler
Genre	F	F	F	F	F
Time	25 min.	35 min.	40 min.	30 min	20 min
Good book So far ?	yes ☑ / no ☐	yes ☑ / no ☐	yes ☑ / no ☐	yes ☑ / no ☐	yes ☐ / no ☐
Time Gole	Times II	Times III	Times II	Times I	All togethe 8

Students created logs to match their individual goals as readers.

Status-of-the-Class Forms

Status-of-the-class forms help us keep track of our students' independent reading on a day-to-day basis. By calling each student's name, asking him to tell us the title of the book and the page number on which he will start, and recording that information, we can look back to see whether he is reading the same book, how much he read, or whether he started reading a new book. We also use this time to ask quick questions to assess. For example, if we notice a student is reading a different book, we will ask, "What happened to the book you were reading yesterday?" If a child has just discovered a new series, we might ask whether she plans to read others in that series. These questions give us lots of information about our students and let us begin conversations that continue at conference times during the reading workshop.

> Kids who
> have quit books
> recently
>
> Meggie
> Brennen
> Hayte
> John
> Madeline

This is a sticky note that Franki used after one status-of-the-class confer-ence. She noticed that some students had a change in their reading behavior, and jotted down students with whom she wanted to meet.

Home Reading Logs

We struggle every year with the question of whether to have students fill out logs for the reading they do at home. On one hand, we want students to read at home because they want to, not because it's required. On the other hand, we know that some students won't read at home until they build the habit, and the home reading log helps them do that. The value of a home reading log is in the conversations it often sparks at home and at school.

Encouraging Conversations Around Home Reading Logs

One year, after students were accustomed to using home reading logs, Franki used the logs as a basis of weekly conversations. Occasionally, she would give students a reflection form to help them think through their home reading. Then she would share some material from these forms with the class.

For example, upon reviewing the forms, Franki realized that many of the students were not reading the same book at home as they were at school. She was concerned because many of these students had enough trouble keeping track of just one book. She looked through logs and found two or three students who *were* reading the same book at home as they were at school. She asked these students to share how that was working for them in the next day's mini-lesson. This started a conversation about the advantages of reading the same book at home and school, and more students were willing to give it a try.

While reflecting on his home reading log, Chris realized that he read the beginning of a book slower than when he got into the book because he was trying to make sense of the story, figure out who the characters were, and understand the setting. Franki knew that paying attention to reading behaviors supports comprehension, so she asked Chris to talk about his revelation with the class. This became one more reading behavior the students could talk about and think about when reflecting on their reading.

Name Chris   Date 10-4

Look over your home and school reading logs so far this year.

What do you notice about your school reading? List 3-5 things.

I notised that I read allot each week.
I also notised that I read diffrent books each week.
I notised That I didnt read as much when I first started a book

What do you notice about your home reading? List 3-5 things.

I notised that I usily read a lot.
I notised that I read about a book a week.
I notised that I mostly read fiction.

How have you changed as a reader this year?

I have gotten better as a reader

What are you most proud of in your reading so far this year?

I am most proud of reading more books

What would you like to improve on in your reading?

I need to finish about a book a week at school.

Chris's home reading log reflection.

Planning for Vacation Reading

One year, after meeting with students in conferences, Franki discovered that many of her students wanted to read longer books. As a reader, she knew she had to make sure to save the longer books for times in her life when she had a little extra reading time. So she brought in books she was saving for vacation. She told students that she would need a few hours to get into such long books, which vacation could provide. She asked if students had any books they were saving for a less busy time of the year. Reading during school vacations is critical to maintaining stamina.

Another year, while talking about her own reading in a mini-lesson, Franki realized that her students didn't have any reading plans for winter vacation. So about a week before break, Franki asked each child to share a book he or she had read—not one that everyone knew, but one that might be new to most classmates. The students spent about an hour sharing good books and writing down the titles of books they might like. Then she asked students to write down their plans for vacation reading. Franki continued lessons like this to encourage reading over long periods of time off from school, such as summer vacation, spring break, and long weekends. As adult readers, we often go to the bookstore or library right before a vacation to stock up. These lessons gave her students the opportunity to do the same thing.

Maria

Summer Reading Plan

Which books have you heard about that you may want to read?
-Half Magic
• Ginger Pye

Which authors have you enjoyed this year?
• Lemony Snicket.

Which genres do you seem to like right now?
• Fiction
• Mystery

Is there a book or kind of book that you didn't have time to read this year that you'd like to read this summer?
• The Grim Grotto

Do you have a goal for your summer reading?
Yes. To read 7 books this summer.

When will you be able to read over the summer?
• Plane to disney.
• Relax time at disney.
• Before bed.

Maria's summer reading plan.

Observations

Because we meet with students in small groups or conferences during independent reading, we aren't always aware of everything that's happening around us and we often miss important things that the other children are doing. So we make time to simply watch students as they read. We grab a pencil and a sticky note and "kidwatch" (Goodman, 1978). In a recent article in the *Council Chronicle*, Heidi Mills states, "Teachers who really engage in careful kidwatching—and don't just think about what they are supposed to teach—focus first on 'who is this child in front of me or this group of kids in front of me, what are their strengths, what strategies are they currently employing, and what is the logical next move for me to make to help them continue to grow?'" (2007, p. 17). If a student has been having trouble finding books, we watch to see whether he is engaged during independent reading. If he is not, we know we need to scaffold his book choice. We would consider a similar approach in the case of the following behaviors:

- Students get up to move around often.
- Students stop to share something from their reading with a friend.
- Students get up to choose a new book several times in one sitting.
- Students take breaks, even though they don't move around the room.
- Students laughing or acting out in other ways while reading.

We may call students over to conference if we notice that they are having trouble finding a book. Or we may look back at the status of the class to see, for example, if a child who frequently switches books has been doing a lot of that lately. We may jot a note when we notice a typically unengaged child laughing out loud at his first Captain Underpants book.

All of this information informs our instruction. Sometimes mini-lessons come from these observations. Other times, we notice behaviors that we can bring up later at an individual conference. For example, when Franki noticed that several kids stopped to share lines from the new Clementine books with others who had read them, she realized that it was time to start book talks so students would have a regularly scheduled time and place to share. When Franki noticed that Molly sometimes stopped to read a picture book in the middle of a chapter book, she asked for a conference. She learned that this was a strategy that worked for Molly. She would stop to read a short familiar book when she found that she was no longer engaged in the longer, unfamiliar book. Then she would return to that book. Molly discovered that strategy on her own and it helped her to finish more books. Franki could have easily asked Molly to stick with one book. Instead, she and Molly talked honestly and learned something fascinating about Molly as a reader.

Students Who Have Trouble Engaging in Books

We are patient at the beginning of the school year, giving students time to settle in, find books they enjoy, and fall in love with reading. We aren't picky about the books they choose or too oncerned about whether the books are right for them. Our priority is getting them into the habit of reading a book for 30 minutes per day. Period. Once those first six weeks are over, most students easily accomplish this, but not all of them.

We pay attention to students who quit books or become restless. When we see this happening, we meet with the student to determine why. Sometimes, it is a comprehension issue; the child can't keep the story clear in her mind. For some students, the beginning of the book is confusing, and they can't understand it. As a result, they are not getting critical information they need to understand the rest of the book. Others may have made a poor book choice or may have lost interest in their choice. Our conferences help.

Students Who Lack Stamina

We recently added books on tape to our classroom library because they support students who need to build stamina. Many audiobooks are recorded by actors who do an amazing job of bringing the material to life. Most of these tapes follow the book word for word, so students can follow along as they listen. Playaways are portable digital audiobooks that don't require any outside equipment. Both are great options for our students. For example, last year, Franki had a student, Justin, who wanted to read books that were too difficult for him. Justin stuck with the books, even though he did not always comprehend them. Franki recognized that his reading level did not match his interest level, which made it difficult for him to choose books. She suggested that Justin listen to a book on tape so he could experience books at his interest level. Books on tape are easier to stick with, and they build stamina. Franki continued to work with Justin on reading books successfully on his own at other times of the day, but the book on tape enabled him to enjoy books that interested him.

We certainly do not limit the use of books on tape to our struggling readers. Books on tape have been helpful to many of our students, regardless of their level of proficiency. Many of us, as adults, enjoy books on tape, after all.

Reasons for Using Books on Tape

Books on tape are great for students who:

- Have a comprehension level higher than their fluency level
- Can't seem to finish a book
- Can't find books that interest them
- Are going on a long car trip but can't read in the car
- Continually want to read books that are too difficult

Students Who Choose Books That Are Too Difficult

Every year, we have students who choose books that are too difficult for them. As a result, they are not engaged or fully comprehending what they read. This tells us we need to do some teaching.

We've found that conversations about choosing appropriate books don't work because these students are often trying to prove to others and to themselves that they are ready for challenging books. Reading becomes a status symbol. Conferences usually don't work either, because these students feel the pressure to be reading the same kinds of books as their peers. So we address this concern in whole-class mini-lessons in which we do the following:

- Take a break in our typical, more challenging read-aloud and move to a book from a series that would be more appropriate for this child, like Horrible Harry. Since these books are quick reads and will appeal to others in the class, they provide an easy way for the child who is choosing difficult books to see a new possibility.
- Highlight lots of books that are more appropriate with the whole class.
- Gather appropriate books on tape and share them with the class.

Concluding Thoughts

We want our students to become lifelong readers. We encourage them to use independent reading time to develop habits and behaviors that they can use for a lifetime. We also want independent reading to be a joyful time of the day. As we assess our students, we are not only looking at the skills they are developing as they read independently, but also at the ways in which they are gaining independence. In the next chapter we discuss read-aloud and the impact it has on the lives of the readers in our classrooms.

Chapter 4

Read-Aloud

> "Read-aloud may look like an ordinary event in a typical classroom, but it feels extraordinary when the teacher who is reading is aware of the power of the book and the importance of her role in not only reading to her students, but leading them through the book—using read-aloud as a teaching time."
>
> —Mary Lee Hahn, *Reconsidering Read-Aloud* (2002)

Read-aloud is a time for students to understand what is possible in a book and understand that *they* have the power to uncover its deep meanings. During read-aloud, we can teach strategies that good readers use to make meaning and assess their progress. We gather students in a circle to think deeply about great literature. They have tools, such as their read-aloud notebook, to help them. We have the book we've chosen, and begin to read. It is a great time to pull our best thinking together.

As a high school English student, Franki passed her classes with no problems. She read a few of the assigned classics but never really understood them. She wasn't too worried about it because to her and so many of her classmates, English class was about waiting for the teacher to tell her the answers. Her job was to listen for the theme of the book, the symbols in the book and what they represented, and the characters in the book and how they changed. It never occurred to Franki that she could figure out these things on her own. She read to figure out the basic plot and that was it. We use read-aloud time to prevent this from happening—we support our students in developing their own thinking skills around texts.

We believe that reading aloud examples of all genres is important. But because we read aloud so much nonfiction during content time, during reading workshop we read aloud fiction almost exclusively. If our students can learn to understand literary elements and literary analysis in read-aloud, chances are, they will be able to do that on their own when they read in middle and high school literature classes. By showing students how to be flexible in their thinking, we give them power over the text. They will be able to approach any text with confidence and skill. Here are some of the things we do in read-aloud to accomplish these goals:

- Preview the text together
- Create anchor charts to support thinking and talking
- Use read-aloud notebooks and sticky notes
- Hold on to threads of thinking as we read
- Linger over the book by thinking about big questions
- Write responses to read-aloud

By using all of these strategies together, students can become successful readers of fiction. Our goal is for students to build their strategies so that they can be deep readers of complex texts. However, since we can't expect all students to develop at the same pace, read-aloud can support students wherever they may be on the continuum of reading proficiency.

Assessing During Read-Aloud

During read-aloud, we are always monitoring student progress. We do not necessarily focus on their understanding of the book itself. Instead, we look at the ways in which students are thinking about reading strategies with deeper understanding. As we listen and observe, we look for strengths and challenges, and support students as they move toward independence.

It's important to remember that students in grade 3 to 6 have only been reading chapter books for a very short time. It is a big leap to move from the Junie B. Jones series to young adult novels. Because instruction in the early grades focuses on books with clear, easy-to-follow plots, students understand what is happening in the story and can predict what will happen next. But in later grades, plots become more complicated, more character driven. The author may use sophisticated techniques, such as flashbacks and foreshadowing, or may present subtle, interrelated themes, instead of one obvious theme. Students in the intermediate grades will be more thoughtful readers if they are invited to think more deeply about things like this.

Choosing Books for Read-Aloud

Choosing books for read-aloud is one of our favorite things to do. It is tempting to always choose our favorite authors, genres, and titles. It is also tempting to choose books in August for the entire year and just move down the pile. But if we listen to our students during read-aloud, we quickly realize that's not the best approach. Whenever we read a book, our students show how they're making sense of text by the comments they make in whole-class conversations and in their read-aloud notebooks. These comments help guide our selection of the next book for read-aloud. So book choice is cumulative, based on students' interests, observations, and needs.

That is not to say that we choose from scratch every time we read aloud. We do build a list of possibilities each year. We spend much of our free time keeping up with new children's books, reading books that students love, and rereading old favorites. We often start the school year with 15 to 20 titles that we *might* read to our students. Then, as the year goes on, we modify the list. Each class is different, each conversation is different, each reader's notebook is different, and therefore each read-aloud list must be different.

Keeping up with new books is critical. We visit bookstores often, read reviews on the Internet, and talk to others about books. We try to break out of our comfort zones and choose different books each year for read-aloud. Of course, there are those tried-and-true books that we read because history shows intermediate students love them. But we don't read them *every* year because we have found that when we have read a book several times our own thinking begins to color the discussion. It is hard to help students who are reading for the first time what we know so well. We often forget to credit our deep understanding of the book to the multiple times we've read it, or we subconsciously try to re-create the conversation that we had with a previous class instead of creating new thinking with the current class. So we try to have enough great books on our list of possibilities to avoid much repetition.

Our role, as teachers, is to choose books that work for *all* students in our classroom. Some students are just beginning to read chapter books and follow a story over several days. Other students in the class can go beyond the plot and consider themes, analyze characters, and think about symbolism. We always want stories with clear, easy-to-follow plots as well as some complex literary issues. We look for short chapter books with lots to talk about, like *How to Steal a Dog* (O'Connor, 2007) and *Wing Nut* (Auch, 2005).

Possible Books for Read-Aloud

- ***Wing Nut*** by M. J. Auch
- ***The Book Without Words*** by Avi
- ***The Destiny of Linus Hoppe*** by Anne-Laure Bondoux
- ***The Report Card*** by Andrew Clements
- ***Because of Winn-Dixie*** by Kate DiCamillo
- ***The Tale of Despereaux*** by Kate DiCamillo
- ***The Tiger Rising*** by Kate DiCamillo
- ***Knight's Castle*** by Edward Eager
- ***Marshfield Dreams*** by Ralph Fletcher
- ***Spinning Through the Universe*** by Helen Frost
- ***Dragon Rider*** by Cornelia Funke
- ***Olive's Ocean*** by Kevin Henkes
- ***A Mouse Called Wolf*** by Dick King-Smith
- ***The Outcasts of 19 Schuyler Place*** by E. L. Konigsburg
- ***The View From Saturday*** by E. L. Konigsburg
- ***A Wrinkle in Time*** by Madeline L'Engle
- ***The Lion, the Witch and the Wardrobe***, by C. S. Lewis
- ***Baby*** by Patricia MacLachlan
- ***Journey*** by Patricia MacLachlan
- ***Touching Spirit Bear*** by Ben Mikaelsen
- ***The Van Gogh Café*** by Cynthia Rylant
- ***The Bad Beginning*** by Lemony Snicket
- ***Crash*** by Jerry Spinelli

Sometimes, we want every child to have a copy of the book. We do this for several reasons. We want students to begin to use tools other than the read-aloud notebook to track thinking over time. By having copies of the book, students can more easily go back into the text to find evidence to support their thinking. They can also mark and go back to lines that may add up to some bigger understanding. For example, Franki thought each student needed a copy of *Holes* (Sachar, 1998) so that they could easily see the white space between passages, which signals a switch to a new story line. We give students a copy of the book so they can notice features or mark and track thinking. For example, some students tracked any references to flying when *Flying Solo* (Fletcher, 1998) was read aloud. We hope students find ways to mark and look back at text to support thinking.

During read-aloud, students see the possibilities of coming together as a group to think and talk about books. They see ways in which our thinking grows when we put it together. They see the power of books and the power of their own thinking.

Short Novels for Read-Aloud

We often look for short, thoughtful novels that support students in reading beyond plot. This helps them to see lots of possibilities in books in a short time.

- *Wing Nut* by M. J. Auch
- *The Report Card* by Andrew Clements
- *Because of Winn-Dixie* by Kate DiCamillo
- *The Tiger Rising* by Kate DiCamillo
- *Spinning Through the Universe* by Helen Frost
- *Olive's Ocean* by Kevin Henkes
- *Toys Go Out* by Emily Jenkins
- *Kira-Kira* by Cynthia Kadohata
- *Gossamer* by Lois Lowry
- *Baby* by Patricia MacLachlan
- *Journey* by Patricia MacLachlan
- *Boris* by Cynthia Rylant
- *The Van Gogh Café* by Cynthia Rylant
- *Amber Was Brave, Essie Was Smart* by Vera Williams

Encouraging Students to Think During Read-Aloud

A book is challenging for most readers when it has layers of meaning and complex structures. We want our students to understand the theme of a story and sophisticated relationships between characters, but we can't expect students to understand these facets of reading without some support.

When sharing our own insights into a text, it's tempting to focus on the ideas *we* understand about a book, but we must resist the easy route and give

Books With Good Tables of Contents

We post an enlarged copy of the table of contents to invite students to use chapter titles to make better predictions.

- *Ivy and Bean Break the Fossil Record* by Annie Barrows
- *The City of Ember* by Jeanne DuPrau
- *The Toothpaste Millionaire* by Jean Merrill

students tools to make sense of it for themselves. We often read a text three to five times before we share it with a group of students. Is it worthwhile for us to share our in-depth knowledge with students who are hearing the book for the first time? Is it fair for us to expect them to understand it at the same level an adult reader would? We don't want to teach them to wait for the teacher to tell them what they think, rather than realizing the power of their own thinking.

Previewing the Text Together

When we preview a book that we plan to read aloud, we read the book cover, the inside flap, and the first page. For students new to chapter books, this procedure can help build a framework for comprehending the text, making predictions, familiarizing themselves with characters, and getting comfortable with an author's writing style. Previewing builds the foundation of our understanding as we read.

Our hope is that students begin to transfer the previewing skills that we teach in read-aloud to independent reading. It's important to preview in a way that meets the needs of a diverse range of readers. The preview can help students who are just beginning to think about story elements to stretch their thinking. For the more sophisticated readers, the preview provides information and ideas that support their understanding of the story during the read-aloud. All readers use what they learn in the preview to add a deeper understanding to the text.

For the first several weeks of school, we read short books so we can cover a variety of topics and genres in a short amount of time. We listen for how the students use the preview to talk about those books. What we hear helps us identify the students who can transfer what they learn in the preview to the reading of the entire book. We observe behaviors that help us understand which students will need a lot of support and which ones won't.

Once the first six weeks are over, we want the level of talk to become more thoughtful. One year, Franki noticed that the preview conversation seemed to get stale. The conversation around the first two books helped students become familiar with the routine, but by the third book it was not revealing deep thinking by the students. Although they were talking about the book, the talk wasn't getting any richer.

How do we know if talk is getting richer? We ask ourselves several questions:

- Are students moving beyond comfortable predictions?
- Are students taking risks and changing their thinking?
- Are students finding new ways to keep track of their thinking in their notebooks?
- Are students thinking deeply about one issue or are they jumping around in their thinking and talking?

Early one year, Franki felt many students were ready to think about themes and issues over the course of a whole book because their conversations during the reading of previous books showed hints of a deeper understanding. So Franki chose *Journey* (MacLachlan, 1991) for the next read-aloud. As usual, she passed out a preview packet that included a copy of the cover of the book, the back cover, the author blurb, the quotes at the beginning of the book, and the first page of chapter 1. Franki talked to students about their predictions and thoughts following the preview, and they began to develop a foundation for understanding the whole book.

When previewing becomes part of every read-aloud, students notice many details that help them understand the book. They come to expect that everything in the book is there for a reason. Late in the year, the class did a preview of *Dragon Rider* (Funke, 2005), a book Franki had not previously read. Franki's students wanted her to experience the story with them for the first time. The book included a foldout map that a reader would most likely look at when previewing the book. Franki mentioned that the foldout map in the book seemed like a waste to her and wondered why the publisher didn't just put it on the end pages or in the middle of the book. Franki was met with several disapproving glares. Sam said, "Mrs. Sibberson, there is probably a reason for the map. We just don't know it yet. We'll have to hold on to the information on the map as we read." After closer examination, the students noticed that there were some words on the map and continued to discuss its importance throughout the read-aloud. Sam helped Franki realize that she needed to suspend judgment and discover the reason for the map as the story unfolded.

Franki added this information to Sam's ever-changing profile as a reader and planned to watch for this type of thinking from other students in the class. Suspending judgment and accepting new information that we discover in our reading are important skills for successful readers.

> ## Books With Interesting Text Features
>
> - ◆ **Poppy** by Avi has a map of its setting.
> - ◆ **The City of Ember** by Jeanne DuPrau has a map of the fictitious city.
> - ◆ **Judy Moody Gets Famous** by Megan McDonald has illustrations of the characters on the end pages.
> - ◆ **Inkheart** by Cornelia Funke has a quote at the beginning of each chapter.

Creating Anchor Charts to Support Thinking and Talking

During read-aloud, it's important to capture our thinking in a very visible way. Creating anchor charts is an excellent way to do that because they allow us to extend the preview and whole-class conversations. By revisiting charts together during read-aloud, we broaden our thinking.

Following the preview of *Journey*, Franki and her students created a chart listing questions that seemed worth paying attention to as Franki read the book:

- ◆ How do the quotes at the beginning of the book connect to the story?
- ◆ Does Journey change in the book?
- ◆ Will the theme be similar to that of *Because of Winn-Dixie* (DiCamillo, 2000)?
- ◆ What does the title mean? Is it just the character's name or does it mean something else?

◆ Is the setting important?

◆ How is photography important?

Before read-aloud the next day, Franki wrote each question on a blank chart. She hung the six charts on the board in the read-aloud area, along with several markers. Before she began reading, Franki explained to students that the charts had come from their thinking on the previous day and would help them keep track of their thinking as she read. As Franki read aloud, the class stopped often to think about each question and write any lines from the text that might contain an answer.

Photography

- Photography is a tool for dealing with things everybody knows about but isn't attending to.
- My grandfather is belly down in the meadow with his camera, taking a close up of a cow pie.
- The focus on the picture is me.
- Chapter 2 — The grandma said that he had to take pictures like that.
- He always has his camera.
  "Sometimes the truth is behind the pictures, not in them."

A chart from a read-aloud of *Journey*. Students held on to certain ideas they formulated during the preview.

Recently, Franki's class read *The View from Saturday* (Konigsburg, 1996). Following the preview, Franki asked the class to think about questions they had. As she was recording, she realized that some of their questions were *little questions* that would probably be answered quickly and easily, and some were *big questions* that readers would think about all through the story. Franki wanted her students to see the difference between the two types of questions, and hoped that they'd keep some of these big questions in their heads during the read-aloud. Franki knew that if they focused on the big questions, they would be able to understand the story at a deeper level. Before they began the read-aloud, Franki had the students revisit their original list of questions and put an asterisk next to those questions that they would have to hold on to and think about throughout most or all of the read-aloud. Many students chose one of these questions to track in their notebooks while the book was read.

In the past, we always rushed into starting a new read-aloud book. As a result, the students understood the book only at a basic level because much of their time was spent keeping track of characters, predicting what might happen next, and trying to make sense of where the story was going. But when we started doing previews, students began to make sense of the book even before we started reading, which led to much richer thinking.

Questions About E. L. Konigsburg's *The View From Saturday*

- Why is it called *The View from Saturday?* *
- Why did they choose the cover illustration? *
- Will there be a tea party?
- Do they beat the odds? Does beating the odds mean just winning? *
- What kind of team is it exactly? What kind of competition?
- Who are the team members? *
- Who is the main character? *
- What is the team trying to do in the Academic Bowl?
- What is the theme or big message? *

* big questions to hold onto throughout the book as we read

Using Read-Aloud Notebooks and Sticky Notes

When Franki's class gets together for read-aloud, the students bring their read-aloud notebooks. In their notebooks, they may make a prediction, ask a question, or make connections to other books they've read. Again, Franki does not want to tell her students what to write. Instead she gives them a tool and asks them to share how they use it, often naming it for them ("Oh, you made a prediction based on what we read.") Making predictions is another risk-free way to make meaning of the text.

Similarly, when it is appropriate, Franki gives each student a copy of the read-aloud book and sticky notes for marking places in the text that spark predictions, questions, connections, or thoughts connected to a big question. Sometimes when Franki reads aloud she pauses and asks students to predict what happens in the text. Other times, she pauses to have them write in their notebooks. Her students always have the option of recording their thinking in their read-aloud notebooks or on sticky notes.

After students have had time to use their notebooks and have seen how other students use theirs, they choose to use their notebooks in ways that focus their reading. Some students might follow a character to determine how he or she changes throughout the story. Other students might focus on the book's title and record clues to the reason the author chose the title. Still others might focus on finding the book's main theme by writing down lines that seem to connect to a bigger message.

During the read-aloud of *The Tiger Rising* (DiCamillo, 2001), for example, Franki's class wondered about the title of the book. Early in the reading, several students noticed that the word *rise* came up a few times. Terri decided to record all the times that Kate DiCamillo used the word. As she read, Franki stopped each time someone noticed a form of the word *rise* so Terri could record it. Most students had never thought about a connection between the title and the story. Terri came up with a great strategy for unlocking the title's meaning, and the class learned from her that sophisticated readers pay attention to the underlying significance of words. Terri was developing independence as a reader, so Franki added that fact to her profile. Franki also went on the lookout for other students who picked up the skill.

During the preview for *The View From Saturday*, many students were interested in the dedication. Konigsburg dedicated the book to David, who "beat the odds." During the preview, the students predicted that the dedication could have something to do with the book's theme, and so Justin decided to track instances in the book where someone seemed to beat the odds. Once again, all readers in the class benefited from Justin's strategy, and Franki made note of his progress.

During a reading of Lemony Snicket's *The Bad Beginning* (1999), Maria became intrigued by the meanings of the characters' names. Since Maria knew that this author pays special attention to his choice of words, she was sure that the characters' names were chosen for a reason. She researched the meanings of the names, much as a parent who is choosing a name for a child does, and kept the meanings handy during the reading, which gave her another way to think about the characters. Maria moved toward a more sophisticated perspective of characters by looking for connections between their names and their identities.

Because students are each tracking different things in their notebooks and sticky notes, the whole-class conversations are multilayered. The class stops to talk often, so everyone benefits. Everyone sees how all these things come together. Our read-aloud session includes lots of time to talk about the ways we are using our notebooks to help understand the book.

Franki often keeps a notebook on chart paper to collect lines with powerful language, track character traits and changes, list recurring words, make connections to a quote or epigraph, and list references to the title. Franki often models some part of her thinking that may be new to students to induce them to try it.

Books With Characters That Change Dramatically Over Time

◆ *Crash* by Jerry Spinelli

◆ *The Birthday Room* by Kevin Henkes

◆ *A Single Shard* by Linda Sue Park

◆ *The Year of the Dog* by Grace Lin

◆ *Rules* by Cynthia Lord

Giving Each Student a Copy of the Read-Aloud Book

Every so often, we read aloud a book and make sure that every child in the class has a copy of it. We don't do this often and we don't require students to follow along in their book. Some students comprehend better when following along, while others have more difficulty when they follow along. So we give students a choice.

When we give students their own copies of the read-aloud books, we sometimes give them a zippered plastic bag and a pack of sticky notes as well. They can use their copies to go back into the text to support their thinking. Since this is one of our big goals for students, the more opportunity they have to practice this on their own, the better. By having a copy of the book, they can mark pages that have lines they want to think about or things they notice about a character. This gives them another tool to use. Instead of using the read-aloud notebook, they can actually put sticky notes in the book.

When we read aloud books with unique text features, such as *The Invention of Hugo Cabret* (Selznick, 2007), we want students to have access to a copy of the book.

If a book is hard to follow—maybe a book told in several voices like *The Homework Machine* (Gutman, 2007)—it helps for students to see the text. The same is true for books such as *Holes* (Sachar, 1998), in which the author uses white space to separate the three story lines. We also try to get individual copies of books like *Trial by Journal* (Klise, 2001), a book told through journal entries, news articles, dry-cleaner receipts, court records, and more. Seeing the text is critical.

Assessing the Impact of Notebooks on Student Learning

We don't assess the notebooks themselves because students would begin to write for our approval rather than to expand their thinking. Instead, we have students complete reflection sheets, which encourage them to think about how they are using their notebooks and if what they are doing is helping them as readers. When we review reflection sheets, we can identify who is benefiting from the notebooks and who is not. We can place the students who are not benefiting into a small group to help them find ways to use their notebooks more effectively. We also ask students who are using their notebooks well to share their strategies with others.

> ## Books With Quotes or Epigraphs
>
> These books begin with a quote or epigraph that can help students focus their thinking on theme.
>
> - **A Book Without Words** by Avi
> - **The Tale of Despereaux** by Kate DiCamillo
> - **The View From Saturday** by E. L. Konigsburg
> - **Touching Spirit Bear** by Ben Mikaelsen

Name _Conner_   Date _3|29_

During our read aloud of The Miraculous Journey of Edward Tulane by Kate DiCamillo, you wrote or sketched in your notebook to help you understand the text. What kinds of writing/sketching did you do during the reading and discussion of this book?

I made 3 boxes on one page. Through dark and darker. How does edward get lost. and Thinking nexts page. What the chariters are doving.

How did writing/sketching help your thinking and understanding of the book?

Through dark and darker
It helps because I vanted to know vhat it meantanel I got thinke that vould help know vhat it meant

What the chariters are doving
It helps because I like to know vhat they are doving what moved that are in anel Other things.

What might you try new in your notebook for one of our next read alouds? Did you see anyone do anything that might work for you?

I think I might us the same thing that I did in this book like What the chariters are doving.

A variety of sheets used for read-aloud reflections.

The Bad Beginning 8-31

I think it is a ship.
or smock. The man calls
Mr. Poe and takes the
childern.

9-1-04

I think Mr. Oloff
will be mean and Albert
and his brother well
wonk for him.

9-2-04

I think the children
tryff to escape, but Count
Oloff can see them from
the tower. The children
borrowed a book for
every week.

9-3-04

I think Justice strac
lates them sleep over.
There snops. I think they
will get dronk and
rob the bank.

9-7-04

If he robs the bank.
If he's spying? I

Name Cole   Date 1-11

Choose one page or entry from your reading notebook. Find one that you are
especially proud of because your writing and thinking really helped you to understand
something better. Explain below why you chose this entry. Be specific.

In the Bad Beginning I started
to draw pictures on the side
of the page to help me. Then
I learned by doing this it
helped me think of where
and what there doing. I also
learned what might happen
next. It also thaught me
how to picture it in my mind
so I could make a good
prediction! I learned that
it also made me think more
about the story.

Reflection sheets ask students simple questions about how they have used their notebooks, as well as deeper questions about how the notebook is supporting their understanding of the book and how they might use strategies in the future. When students fill out reflection sheets, we want to make sure that they are focusing on their understanding. Even when students write in great detail in their notebooks, it doesn't necessarily mean they're exploring their predictions, questions, or connections as deeply as they could be. The reflection sheet is the best assessment.

Another way that we assess how students are using notebooks is by sitting between two students each day during read-aloud. When students stop to write, we glance over at their notebooks to observe. We also engage them in conversations and listen in on what they say. By watching them in the acts of writing and talking, we can assess whether notebooks are working for each child.

Franki sits near different students each day as a way to make informal assessments.

When Notebooks Don't Support Understanding

Even when we choose the perfect book and students are using their notebook and sticky notes, there's no guarantee it will lead to deeper understanding. Scaffolding is critical.

For example, Franki recently read the Newbery Honor book *Rules* (Lord, 2006), the story of a girl who has an autistic brother and is struggling with her various roles and needs related to his condition. The book was quite a hit and the conversations throughout the reading of the book were amazing. The students had very little experience with or knowledge about autism going into the read-aloud, but not coming out of it. Many students mentioned how this book changed the way that they understood people and families who were different from their own. One student mentioned said that during a recent trip to the mall, he saw a family struggling with their autistic son's behavior. He had a new understanding of what they were going through and told me, "I made sure not to stare because I know how that would make them feel now."

But Franki was concerned that analyzing text for theme, character development, and author's craft was challenging for these students. She knew her next book choice would be critical in building these skills. When she looked back at students' notebooks for *Rules*, this concern was confirmed. She found that many of them were jotting down ideas that really didn't help them think critically about the text. They were summarizing the story and sketching characters but weren't getting the larger message of the story. This general assessment prompted Franki to think about how she could encourage students to go deeper into the story. She also realized the topic of autism was so new to them that the depth of the story may have been secondary for her students.

On another occasion, Sydney asked why it was important to write in her read-aloud notebook at all during read-aloud. She had done a lot of thinking about it and didn't know why she needed to write anything down. Franki described an experience she had recently had with a book she was reading. She had been noticing something in the story that seemed to be part of a pattern. When she wanted to go back and look for the pieces of the pattern, she struggled to find them in the text because she hadn't marked the text or written them down as she read. Franki told her that when a reader writes thoughts down and looks at them all together, sometimes new thoughts and understandings emerge. Sydney seemed to accept this new possibility and was willing to give writing in her notebook a shot. This type of honest conversation is critical for assessment-based instruction.

Moving Toward Deeper Understanding

Franki chose *The Miraculous Journey of Edward Tulane* (DiCamillo, 2006) for the next read-aloud for several reasons. The book was short so it wouldn't take long to read, but had many layers of meaning. There was potential for spending a good deal of time talking about the big messages. The class had read *The Tale of Despereaux* (DiCamillo, 2006) by the same author, so Franki hoped students would make some connections between the two books. She also knew that the content of *The Miraculous Journey of Edward Tulane* would be easier to understand than *Rules*. She was confident that most of her students would easily be able to follow the plot and then extend their learning through talking and writing.

Since Franki never tells students what to track or mark, the preview conversation needed to engage them in lots of interesting thinking. She planned to have them focus on questions that would enable them to hold on to an idea in their notebooks. Franki prepared for the preview by copying the cover of the book, the front and back jacket flap, the epigraph, and the first page of chapter 1. She gave students 20 to 30 minutes to look over the preview packet and write down any questions that might help them as they read the book.

Note from Annie
(prepar to cry)

Why dose a bilence heart gets broken

Why dose his heart break?

The heart breaks and breaks
and lives by breaking.
It is necessary to go
through dark and deeper dark
and not to turn.

Why is it necessary?

Why not turn?

—from "The Testing-Tree," by Stanley Kunitz

M   his jorney might get dark

M   A bilence gets heartbroken when
Edward gets lost

e - evidence

M - Maybe

K - Know

Q - questions

What jorney is edward going to mane?
Why did they name him edward Tolane?
What is connected to the tale of despero?

he lived on
egypt street

made of some real
Rabbit fur

china doll

ONCE, IN A HOUSE ON EGYPT STREET, there lived a rabbit who was made almost entirely of china. He had china arms and china legs, china paws and a china head, a china torso and a china nose. His arms and legs were jointed and joined by wire so that his china elbows and china knees could be bent, giving him much freedom of movement.

His ears were made of real rabbit fur, and beneath the fur, there were strong, bendable wires, which allowed the ears to be arranged into poses that reflected the rabbit's mood— jaunty, tired, full of ennui. His tail, too, was made of real rabbit fur and was fluffy and soft and well shaped.

5

Alex's notes on the preview pages from *The Miraculous Journey of Edward Tulane.*

Following their independent previewing, the students came together to talk about what they learned and listed all their questions. Franki used this discussion as a quick way to assess the kinds of thinking the students were doing individually and as a class. She was happy to see the variety of thinking and the potential for great whole-class conversations. Although some questions were plot oriented, focusing on predictions, and others clearly showed confusion, charting the questions helped Franki to see where the class's thinking was.

Questions Raised During Previewing

- How does he get lost?
- How does he have fur and china?
- How do her two books connect? By themes of darkness, journeying, broken hearts?
- How can you give a rabbit freedom?
- What does the quote mean to the story?
- Where does he go on his journey?
- Where is he going on the cover?
- Why is his heart broken?

- Is he alive?
- Why did the girl adore him so much?
- Why did she name him Edward Tulane?
- Why is the street named Egypt Street?
- Why is it necessary to go through dark?
- What does the title tell us?
- How did he live if his heart was broken?
- Will someone faint?
- Will the author talk to us?

On the following day, the students looked back at the questions and thought about the questions and ideas they might want to hold on to during the reading of the book. This time, Franki gave them extra time to think about how they might set up their notebook page to support that. Students spent an entire read-aloud time thinking about things like whether to use columns or boxes and what to focus on. They wrote Franki a quick note, letting her know how this setup would help them understand the text better. This served two purposes. First, it would give students, especially struggling students, the time they needed to carve out a plan to use their notebooks effectively. Second, it would give her a way to assess whether they could use their notebooks to support understanding.

Another year, Franki had students go back into their reader's notebooks to find a page that had really helped them understand something in the text. By doing this, students were able to see when writing helped and when it did not. She used these pages in mini-lessons over several days and had students share notebook pages that supported their thinking as readers. To support students throughout the year, she posted these samples and explanations on a board in the room and invited students to try new strategies in their notebooks. Sometimes sharing successful strategies is all that is needed to push students' thinking forward.

Rohith

I have a small box for when I find something related to the tale of desperaux because I don't think I will find much stuff that are related to the book. I am actually going to make the Thought about Edwards bigger but I didn't have space. I am probably going to have a lot of questions about it Edward and dubeline so I made it big I think I am going to hear a lot of words from the quote so I made it big to write the sentence. I made predictions big because I think I am going to make a lot of predictions.

Rohith

Questions	Predictions
When I find something related to the tale of des Peraux	every time I hear a word in the quote
Thoughts about Edward	

Students set up their read-aloud notebooks in different ways to help them think more deeply about the book.

Day-to-Day Assessment in the Reading Workshop

Note book   3/14

The miraculous jurney of
Edward Tulane

Keeping track of mood

	Mood	Sentence/words	Chapter #
example →	Happy	Abilene hugged Edward tightly.	#4

Sruti

The miraculas jurney Letter 3/14
of Edward Tulane

I want to keep track of what mood Edward is in so I can see If he is more happier or sad because last time I read the book I couldn't really tell so that is why I am doing that. I put the Chapter # because I thought I would See when he gets happy or sad. I made the middle box bigger because I can have more space to write the sentence or words. I think that when we start I will I will get to know Edward Tulane much better.

The Jacket

(handwritten student notebook pages displayed on a bulletin board)

The outcasts of 19 schuyler Place

Students identified places where the read-aloud notebook was effective for understanding the text. These were posted for other students to examine.

Inviting Students to Use Literary Terms to Discuss Characters

"Most students consider the formal study of literary devices the epitome of school for school's sake. They contend that nobody apart from the occasional English teacher cares a jot about figures of speech. What they don't understand is that understanding how literary devices work gives readers power over text. The more clearly students understand how a writer works his magic in a line of poetry or prose, the better they will be able to analyze the line."

—Carol Jago, *Classics in the Classroom: Designing Accessible Literature Lessons* (2004)

To help students understand vocabulary that will lead them to think more deeply about text and to raise the level of conversation, we sometimes display literary terms on the board. For example, one year Franki noticed that much of the conversation around *The Book Without Words: A Fable of Medieval Magic* (Avi, 2005) centered around the characters in the book, so Franki seized the opportunity to give her students a specific way to think about characters more deeply. She introduced the terms that readers use to describe different characters, such as *antagonist, protagonist*, *round character*, *flat character*, *static character*, and *dynamic character*, and displayed them on a chart in the read-aloud area. Franki was not mandating that students learn these terms. Rather, she was inviting them to use a common language to think about characters in more in-depth ways.

Usually, this invitation is all students need to start trying out the terms in their book talk. In the read-aloud conversation about *The Book Without Words*, students seemed to ignore the terms for a few days, but on day three, Brett piped up and said one of the characters was the antagonist. All of the terms became part of the classroom talk from that point on.

Lingering Over the Book by Thinking About Big Questions

"You can also show students that a readers notebook can be a place to stay with an idea for a long time. For example, if a child gets the idea from a book that elderly people are wise and often teach young people, he might follow and grow that idea for many months and across several books."

—Janet Angelillo, *Writing About Reading: From Book Talk to Literary Essays, Grades 3–8* (2003)

One way that we help students see beyond the plot is to have them think about big questions after we are finished reading—questions they are interested in pondering in small groups over a few days. We spend a great deal of time discussing the difference between little questions (those that have answers in the text, such as "How old is Catherine in *Rules*?") and big questions (those with no clear-cut answer, but which inspire rich thinking and discussion, such as "How did Journey's relationship with his grandfather change and why?").

After finishing a read-aloud book, we chart big questions that we'd like to think and talk about. Students look over the chart and decide on the question they'd like to discuss. They then get into groups with others who are interested in the same question. It doesn't matter which big question they choose because any question that is truly a big question will help them delve more deeply into the book. By asking them to stick with one question, we encourage students to build their thinking through talk and continue to think of new angles. This helps them understand that a book isn't over when you finish the last page. The best readers linger over a book.

When Franki's class finished *The Tale of Despereaux*, one group lingered over the meaning of light and dark in the book. They tracked all the places where DiCamillo used these two words. Then they analyzed the dark and light traits of each character to define each word in the context of the book.

During the discussion of *Journey*, one group became interested in the role of photography in the book. Franki read a quote about photography during the preview before reading the book itself. From there, the students went back to look at all the references to photography and to think about its significance to the story.

Following the reading of *The View From Saturday*, the chart included these big questions:

- What is the theme/big message?
- What does the title mean? What does "view" in the title mean?
- Why did the author choose the characters' names?

- Why was tea so important?
- What does "beating the odds" from the dedication mean in the book?
- What is the connection between Humpty Dumpty and Mrs. Olinski?
- Why are the turtles mentioned so often?
- What is the meaning of the line "And that was when she knew that they knew that she knew" on page 160?
- Why did it win the Newbery Medal?
- What does the front cover illustration mean?
- Who is the main character?

Students were particularly curious about the cover illustration of *The View From Saturday*. One group spent several days discussing the illustrations and how they might refer to the text.

Charting big questions after a reading always gives us a great deal of information. So does listening to students discuss those questions. How students think about a book after reading it says a lot about how they are approaching text. We learn about individual students (Is there a lot of confusion about the text?) and we learn about the class in general (Do class discussions show a deeper understanding of text?)

After reading the book *Rules*, Franki realized that none of the big questions focused on character development. Yet analyzing characters and the changes that occur in characters is critical for students. So, for her next read-aloud, she chose Jerry Spinelli's *Crash* (1996), which has an engaging plot based on two multifaceted characters. Franki knew that the book would naturally lend itself to thinking and talking more deeply about characters.

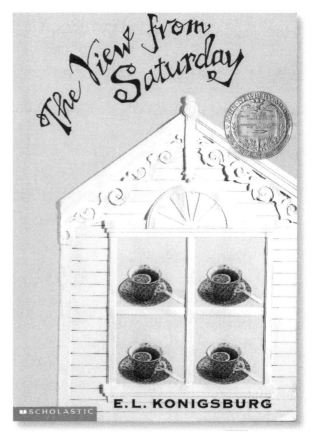

After the class read *Because of Winn-Dixie*, Franki shared some questions that appeared in a guide that accompanies the movie adaptation of the book. She and the students talked about which questions were worth discussing and which were not. By looking at the various questions in the guide, the class learned to pinpoint the characteristics of questions that are worth talking, thinking, and writing about.

Big questions seem to impact students' independent reading as well. Instead of finishing a book and moving on, students linger with books during independent reading well beyond the last page. This time to think deeply about the book has been powerful for all students.

Writing in Response to Read-Aloud

"Once we can get children to comprehend and respond thoughtfully to texts in conversation and in short jottings to record their thinking, we can then work on the muscles of writing well in authentic genres of writing about reading. But we should not expect that children will be able to do the writing work until we have heavily scaffolded their thinking and note-taking, as well as their organizing and planning of their writing."

—Janet Angelillo, *Writing About Reading: From Book Talk to Literary Essays, Grades 3–8* (2003)

Mei
May 5.

The question I studied was, how does each character have a little owl in them? The 4 main characters, Roy, Dana, Mullet Fingers, Beatrice, and Officer Delinko, all have a little owl in them. Here is my ideas for each characters and their own little owl.

Roy, the main character had an owl in him. I think that because when Roy moved, he wasn't known much in school, but the people started noticing him when he beat up Dana. Same with the owls. No one knew about the owls but when Mullet Fingers stood up for them, everyone was like, owls! What owls? and started going up on Roy's side.

Dana was hard, but we finally came up with something that we all agreed on. Dana has a owl in her because she hid from the police, and the owls are hiding from the bulldozers. Another thing we came up with later for Dana, is also she is the owl chasing Roy, and Roy is sort of like its meal.

Officer Delinko has some owl in him. He

After a class discussion, students write essays following the conversations about the book we've just finished. Each essay reflects a student's thinking on a big idea from the book.

After we've read a book aloud, talked as a whole class, charted some thinking, used notebooks to track thinking, and lingered with big questions in small-group discussions, writing in response to the read-aloud becomes more powerful. Instead of getting responses in which students summarize the book and tell why they like or do not like it, we get responses that show students can think hard about one of the book's central issues.

Méi

has some owl in him because he was sort of shy and hiding from the other more important police officers. The owls were sort of hiding and trying to stay on the good side of other people. The owls and Officer Delinko both wanted to be important but didn't really stand up for themselfs. Officer Delinko wanted People like Roy's Father to stand up for him and write a letter for his files. Mullet Fingers stood up for the owls who needed help.

Mullet Finger had some owl in him because he hids from his mom and the owls hid from the people, police officers, and the bulldozers. Mullet Fingers tries to sneak away and the owls go in and out of their burrows without anyone seeing them.

Beatrice is the last charactor. Beatrice tries to stay away when her mom and dad fight. Same with the owls, they try to stay away when people are around and try not to be seen.

Those are my ideas for each character. The answer to my question, Do all characters have a little owl in them? is a yes. Yes, all characters have a little owl in them. That is what I think.

We encourage students to use one of the big questions they charted (or one that they thought of later) to help focus their writing. Because they have benefited from the thinking of everyone in the class, students feel more confident about the writing. Writing becomes a way to synthesize thinking. We can use this time to teach a great deal about writing in response to reading.

Students begin to realize that writing can invite new thoughts. Often, as students are writing following a read-aloud, Franki asks them to underline passages that demonstrate thinking—thinking that happened *because* they are writing their thoughts down. This is a powerful experience for students.

Writing in response to read-aloud is also a rich form of assessment. It allows us to track the depth of understanding and identify when a student reaches a new level of thinking and understanding.

When Read-Aloud Isn't Going Anywhere

When the read-aloud conversation is flat and contains no spark, we reflect on the reasons why and determine a way to breathe life into it. One winter, Franki had an amazing student teacher named Dan Lowe. Dan was reading *Al Capone Does My Shirts* (Choldenko, 2004), the story of Moose, who moves with his family to Alcatraz when his father gets a job as a prison guard. The year is 1935, and Al Capone is a prisoner there. Moose's sister Natalie is autistic, and this move may allow her to go to a special school close by.

Dan didn't feel like the conversation was going anywhere, so he asked Franki to step in. He'd been in the classroom for some of Franki's read-aloud sessions, so he knew just how lively those conversations could be, and he was disappointed. What he didn't know was that Franki experiences the same sense of disappointment several times each year. Sometimes read-aloud conversations just do not go well. Students seem to just go through the motions. When that happens, we need to stop reading, have honest conversations, problem solve together, and build on our thinking.

Having Honest Conversations

Franki gathered the class together and shared the concern that she and Dan had about that level of the read-aloud conversation. Several students said that the book didn't give them much to think about. Franki focused on the few students who had found some interesting things to think about. Megan said that she was fascinated by the characters and was trying to figure out who the main one was. She was torn between Moose and Natalie, and was jotting things down about each to determine who was the protagonist. Franki reminded the class about words that describe types of characters. (See pages 98-99 for those words.) She asked the students if the list would help them think differently about the characters. Some agreed that it might.

Rebecca said she was interested in Natalie's autism and how it affected her. The group was silent. No thoughts. When this happens, our gut reaction is to just drop the idea, quit the book, and move on. But if we give students time, they usually find more to say. Franki was very honest. She told the students she felt they were not even trying to think deeply about the story and asked them to tell her why. She wanted them to figure this out together.

Problem Solving Together

Franki asked the students to tell her what they were wondering about and started a list of what they shared. Chris was wondering about the prison and what it had to do with the story. It seemed that the setting was important, but he wasn't sure why. Brett wondered about whether or not the mother in the story was being fair. The conversation became silent again, but students seemed far more engaged.

Franki asked Will if anything on the list looked interesting to him. His eyes lit up. He said, "I was just thinking about this. The book might be set in the prison because the characters Moose and Natalie feel imprisoned. It's like one of those metaphors. Moose feels imprisoned because of Natalie and Natalie is a prisoner in herself." The energy surged through the room. A few students oooohed and ahhhed. Everyone was amazed. Franki asked Will how he came up with this idea. He said that he was looking at the list and trying to figure out if there was any connections between his classmates' responses and any of the ideas on the list. He realized that Rebecca's thinking about autism and Chris's thinking about the prison could be connected in this way. So he decided to follow this thread as Franki continued reading.

Will's idea of imprisonment made Maria think of a character from another book she had read, *So B. It* (Weeks, 2005). She decided to pay attention to the similarities of the two characters as Franki continued to read the book. The rest of the class found other threads to follow.

Will's comment brought the energy back to the conversation by inspiring questions like these:

- How can we look at the questions we had in the past and connect them to what we're reading now?
- How can we surprise ourselves with our thinking more often?
- How can these surprises help us think about the bigger messages of the book?

When things aren't going well during a read-aloud, problem solving together is the key to moving conversations forward. Before this conversation, Franki couldn't recognize what was holding students back, so she couldn't help them. Honest conversations such as these enable students and teacher to move forward and avoid playing "the game of school."

Building on Our Thinking

Franki asked the class how the conversation about *Al Capone Does My Shirts* was different from past discussions. She wanted students to think about how and why this conversation had energized their thinking. Maddie said she noticed that her classmates really started to build on one another's thinking again. In the past few weeks, they had fallen back into the habit of talking about their own ideas only. But during this conversation, they listened and tried to merge their ideas. Maddie helped the class recognize the power of collaboration.

Every time one of these high-energy conversations occurs, we hope the lessons learned from it have staying power. Will insights gained about one book support students' understanding of another book? In this case, connecting seemingly unconnected ideas caught on and became a tool students used to think through issues in future reading.

Months later, when Franki read aloud *Hoot* (Hiaasen, 2006), students began talking about the significance of the owls and wondering whether the characters had any owl characteristics. Whether or not this was what the author intended, the connection gave students a new way to think about characters. In an essay she wrote after the read-aloud, Mei wrote, "How does each character have a little owl in them?" We have to remember that each conversation can and should give students new tools for future understanding.

Franki gained insights from each of these conversations as well as new strategies for energizing future conversations. The line between assessment and instruction is especially blurred in these examples. Read-aloud and the conversations we have with students serve both purposes equally. It's a fine balance, knowing when to listen and observe and knowing when to deliver explicit teaching to help our students grow as readers.

What We Might Ask to Build on Conversation

What We Notice:	What We Might Ask:
A student makes a prediction.	What makes you think that?
A student agrees with someone.	Are you building on what Brennen said?
A student makes a new prediction.	What made you change your thinking?
A student comments on a character.	What did the character do or say to make you think that?
A student comments on a character changing.	When do you think he/she started changing?

Concluding Thoughts

Read-aloud is a routine that brings students and teacher together. The discussions that arise help to build the level of conversations about books. Students can come up with their own strategies for making sense out of text. They learn strategies and build knowledge that will help them make sense of texts for a lifetime. In the next chapter, we take a look at how whole-class instruction supports and encourages readers.

Chapter 5

Whole-Class Instruction: Mini-Lessons

> "I want children to see themselves not only as inquiring individuals, but as inquiring individuals who are part of a diverse community that inquires, whose members, through their active participation and diversity of perspective, contribute to each other's intellectual growth."
>
> —Peter Johnston, *Choice Words: How Our Language Affects Children's Learning (2004)*

In reading workshop, we allow students to spend time reading books that are just right for them. We meet with students individually to discuss their unique needs as readers. We gather students who have similar challenges into small groups. In addition, we believe that coming together as a whole group for explicit teaching and informal sharing is critical. We teach whole-class mini-lessons that meet the needs of all students, and those mini-lessons are anchors for our conversations about reading skills, strategies, and behaviors. Sometimes our whole-group instruction time is devoted entirely to explicit teaching, sometimes to informal sharing, and sometimes both.

We don't rely on packaged mini-lessons because they don't take into account our assessments, which are critical to deciding what students need. Although we may use great resources such as *Strategies That Work* (Harvey & Goudvis, 2000) for inspiration, we never follow a sequenced program. Instead, when we plan mini-lessons, we think about our state standards, our students, and what skills and strategies our students need to become independent. Mini-lessons are the most explicit teaching we do. They are focused and brief, built on the conversation that we have every day. As such, students come to realize that they are learning skills and strategies they might use the day we teach them, or they may save them until the need to use them arises. According to Pat Johnson, author of *One Child at a Time: Making the Most of Your Time With Struggling Readers, K–6* (2006), "Many times a reader uses a combination of several strategies that overlap and intertwine. The important point is that these strategies have to be available to the reader so that she may draw upon them flexibly and fluently." (p. 18). In this chapter, we offer ways to help students do just that as well as to assess their progress.

Typical Structure of a Mini-Lesson

- Students usually gather at the easel.
- We begin the lesson by saying something like, "I have noticed that..." We want students to know that the mini-lesson comes from something that has revealed itself in our formal and informal assessments.
- We usually demonstrate the skill or strategy in a conversational way. "When I was reading..."
- We invite students to add their own thinking to the conversation.
- We ask students about their own experiences with the skill or strategy.
- We invite them to pay attention, over the next few days and weeks, to their own reading behaviors as they relate to the mini-lesson, and to tell us what they notice.
- We reflect on student learning and on possible future teaching points.

Determining Topics for Mini-Lessons

Our topics for mini-lessons come from three main sources: the state standards, day-to-day observations in reading workshop, and the results of more formal assessments.

The Required State Standards

Knowing our required state standards plays a huge role in planning whole-class instruction. We make sure we are engaging students in learning experiences that represent all of the standards, while recognizing that each child's journey to meeting those standards is different.

When we look across our state standards, we see many strategies and skills, such as making good predictions, finding important information, and reading a variety of genres. Our mini-lessons must address all areas of the standards. Some mini-lessons focus on strategies for comprehension, such as identifying important information or understanding vocabulary. Other mini-lessons focus on building reader identity and support students in their behaviors as readers. We make sure that we give our students the tools that support them in *all* areas of reading. We balance what students need to learn (the standards) with what we observe them doing in the classroom. We are watchful for areas of learning in which students are struggling and plan mini-lessons to address those areas. We provide a broad range of mini-lessons so children can become independent and successful readers and meet state standards.

Observations in Reading Workshop

Mini-lesson topics also come from what we learn about our students through observation. We pay close attention to what students do and say in all reading workshop routines. And we keep our big goals in mind. Almost every year, we find that students need whole-class help in making predictions, using evidence from the text to support their thinking, and choosing appropriate books for independent reading. However, there are always things that are unique to a class—things that we don't anticipate. We have to be ready to recognize the areas in which our students need instruction and provide experiences that will help them become more independent.

Students internalize and apply what we teach in mini-lessons if the topics come from their daily lives in reading workshop. The lessons become so much more powerful when we can start by saying something like, "I noticed during read-aloud last week that it's challenging for some of you to use the table of contents to support your predictions" or "When I met in conferences with people last week, I noticed that several of you were having difficulty choosing books."

With every piece of assessment data we collect, we look for patterns across the class to help plan our mini-lessons. We listen in on conversations, look at writing in response to

Twelve Typical Mini-Lesson Topics

- Using the text to support thinking and opinions
- Supporting predictions with evidence in the text
- Noticing the things you wonder as you read
- The importance of changing your thinking when new evidence is presented
- Using text features to support understanding
- Ways to build on someone else's thinking in a conversation
- Strategies to help you when you find your mind wandering
- Paying attention to ways characters change over the course of a story
- Finding a place and a time to read at home
- Choosing appropriate books
- Reading a variety of genres
- Talking to others when choosing new books

reflective questions, or talk to students during conferences. When we see only one or two children struggling with a skill or strategy, we use conferring and small-group instruction to meet their needs. But when the majority of students are struggling, we teach a mini-lesson (or a series of mini-lessons) to the whole class.

Children change as readers, and their needs change. So we worry when we see rigid, yearlong plans for mini-lesson topics (book choice in September, the inferring strategy in October, and so forth). Although we sketch out a yearly plan, it's a *very* flexible plan. While we do have some mini-lessons we teach every year, the majority of our lessons do not repeat from year to year. Instead, they reflect what we notice about our students. We plan thoughtfully. We don't teach a mini-lesson until we have assessment data that proves our current students need it.

Holding On to What We Learn About Our Students for Future Teaching

Mini-lesson topics often come from what we see and hear in whole-class conversations or small-group work. For example, Franki's students were discussing *The Summer My Father Was Ten* (Brisson, 1999), the story of a young boy who ruins a neighbor's garden when playing baseball. He later helps the neighbor rebuild his garden and the two become friends. A few students were trying to determine the turning point in the story and agreed it was the moment the boy ruined the garden because the rest of the story could not happen without it. As tempted as she was to jump in and "correct" the students by telling them that the turning point is actually when the young boy began to help the neighbor rebuild his garden, Franki resisted because that would not have empowered students to think through text on their own. She knew that over time and with support, her students would become skilled at identifying the turning point in a story. So Franki made a mental note of the conversation, and planned to teach several mini-lessons over the next few weeks to help children learn to identify the turning point in a story.

For each lesson, she read aloud a picture book with a clear turning point and discussed the important events in the story. By naming and studying important events, particularly the turning point, students developed skills they could use to discuss and write about other books.

> ### Picture Books With Clear Turning Points
> - *The Other Side* by Jacqueline Woodson
> - *Scaredy Squirrel* by Mélanie Watt
> - *Lost and Found* by Oliver Jeffers
> - *Brothers* by Yin
> - *The Royal Bee* by Frances Park and Ginger Park

Weaving Our Lives as Readers into Mini-Lessons

We want our students to know themselves well as readers. We also want them to know their classmates as readers. When we share our personal experiences with books and reading, our students learn that many of the challenges they face are universal. For example, they might not have the stamina to stay with a book because their comprehension breaks down. They may become confused and stop reading. Perhaps they have not made a good book choice. When we notice a struggle like that, we think about our own reading and try to recall a similar experience. Then we share in a mini-lesson how we handled it. Over the years, we've become quite good at paying attention to our own reading lives, knowing that we can later use all that we do as readers in our mini-lessons.

Franki realized that several of her students were stuck in a genre and resisting venturing out to other genres. At the same time, she had just finished *The Other Boleyn Girl* (Gregory, 2004), a book a friend had recommended that she wasn't very excited about initially. She didn't consider herself a reader of historical fiction. But she read it, and it became one of her favorite books of all time. Franki brought the book in to share with her students and told them that since she had never loved historical fiction, she was hesitant to read *The Other Boleyn Girl* at first. She discovered, though, that reading historical fiction could be an enjoyable experience. It was important for students to see that even though Franki had been reading for a long time, her tastes continued to change. As she often does when she finishes a mini-lesson, Franki asked students to pay attention to times when they were open to new kinds of books. She knew this mini-lesson would be the beginning of much longer conversations about the changing tastes of readers, and that it would spark many conversations throughout the year about choosing books. She knew that some students would immediately try a new genre while others would need to live with the idea at first.

Emphasizing Nonfiction

One year, while reviewing reading logs during individual conferences, Franki realized that many of her students had been choosing only fiction. Rather than meeting with students one-on-one, which would has been time-consuming, she gave a mini-lesson in which she elicited ideas from the students about ways to include more nonfiction in their reading repertoire. She began the lesson by saying, "When I was meeting with everyone over the last few weeks, I was so excited about the variety of books you are choosing. So many of you are trying new authors, taking recommendations from friends, and finding favorite series. One thing that I noticed though, was that not many of you are reading nonfiction and I was wondering why."

The students said they don't read nonfiction because they don't like it. Nonfiction was "school-time reading." After her initial panic, Franki considered the negative messages she may have been sending about nonfiction. She knew she had to help her students see themselves as nonfiction readers and to place more value on nonfiction books for pleasure reading. She ended the mini-lesson knowing she'd come back to this issue. After some reflection she planned a series of mini-lessons based on what she had learned from her students.

The Teacher as a Nonfiction Reader

Franki planned to start her mini-lesson by talking about her own interest in nonfiction. As she reflected, she realized that so much of her nonfiction reading included professional books and articles on teaching. She wanted to share this realization, but didn't want to promote the notion that nonfiction reading was only what you do for work. But then she realized that she read certain sections of the newspaper every day, too, such as Arts and Entertainment. She subscribed to several magazines, including *Good Housekeeping* and *Runner's World*. She liked to bake cookies and had several cookie cookbooks that she consults often. She writes e-mail messages to friends and family on a regular basis. She was reading travel guides to plan an upcoming trip to Walt Disney World. She wanted her students to see all of these materials so she brought the stack of them to school.

She began the lesson by saying, "When I started to think about myself as a nonfiction reader, I thought that all of my nonfiction reading was about teaching. I love to read about teaching and I love to find new books about teaching. But when I started to pay attention to my reading, I realized that I do a lot more nonfiction reading every day. Let me show you." Franki then shared the stack with the class, and invited students to think and talk about their lives as nonfiction readers.

Nonfiction Mini-Lessons

Another year, while students were casually reading nonfiction, Franki walked around the room to note their choices. She noticed that most of her students were choosing nonfiction books that had a great deal of information on a page—photos, captions, and lots of running text. So she decided to assess by sitting back and watching students for the entire reading time. The students were all engaged, but many were skimming and scanning as if they were reading gossip magazines. Most of them did not seem to be thinking too deeply about the text. They needed to learn how to navigate the pages to truly take in the information. So Franki devoted many mini-lessons to this and probed during conferences to make sure that what students learned in the lessons was sticking. She asked herself several questions over the next few days:

◆ Why were her students attracted to books with this setup?

◆ Were they using only pictures to gather information?

◆ Were any of them reading narrative nonfiction?

◆ Did they have a purpose for reading?

These questions helped her determine how students were progressing, as well as where she might go next with nonfiction mini-lessons.

Nonfiction Mini-Lesson #1: Sharing Narrative Nonfiction

Franki realized that she had not placed enough value on narrative nonfiction. She felt that narrative nonfiction, like picture book biographies, provided a helpful bridge from fiction to more traditional nonfiction. She hoped that by introducing narrative nonfiction with a mini-lesson, students would choose it more frequently.

Franki began the lesson by saying, "I noticed during nonfiction reading time that many of you are skimming and scanning nonfiction. That is a great strategy for previewing and for locating information. I've noticed that many of the books you've been choosing are set up like a magazine. You read pages and sections of the text, and you don't have to start

> ## Narrative Nonfiction Picture Books
> - *An Egg Is Quiet* by Dianna Hutts Aston
> - *A Seed Is Sleepy* by Dianna Hutts Aston
> - *Pumpkins* by Ken Robbins
> - *It's a Butterfly's Life* by Irene Kelly
> - *You Forgot Your Skirt, Amelia Bloomer* by Shana Corey

at the beginning and read through the book or page. I've got a stack of nonfiction books here that are written more like fiction, so readers can start at the beginning and read to the end. Some of these books can be read in one day and others may take a few days. They are set up so that readers benefit most from reading them front to back." She introduced each of the books to her students and showcased them on a nearby shelf. She read a few aloud over the next few days, demonstrating how easy they are to navigate and, therefore, comprehend and enjoy.

Franki watched over the next few weeks for children who chose narrative nonfiction. In conversations with them she recognized that they were more engaged in reading than they had been and were diving deeper into the topic.

Although some mini-lessons are more explicit, many, like this one, are more like conversations designed to encourage students to think in new ways or develop new skills. They are quick, and typically end with an open invitation to try something new. These lessons are often the first step in teaching sophisticated concepts.

Nonfiction Mini-Lesson #2: Previewing Nonfiction

When deciding on a just-right nonfiction book for independent reading, it is often helpful for students to focus their selections on books that are written and formatted in a way that helps them take in new information. When students struggle with comprehension, a mini-lesson on previewing nonfiction books may help.

Franki started this mini-lesson with a variety of books by Gail Gibbons, Seymour Simon, and other well-known authors of nonfiction for children. She explained to students that one of the goals of previewing nonfiction is to figure out how the information is presented and whether it is a good fit for the reader. Then Franki shared pages from the books, thinking aloud about how the information was presented.

"In this book, *The Kid Who Invented the Popsicle* [Wulffson, 1999], I am noticing that there seem to be lots of short stories and it looks like a chapter book. If I look at the chapter headings, it looks like each chapter is about a different invention. I guess that I would read this like a chapter book."

"*Pigs* [Gibbons, 2000] looks like a simple picture book about pigs. The illustrations are on the top and the text is on the bottom. But, if I look closely, there seem to be labels and notes in the illustrations. This is a book that I would probably read twice. I would read the story on the bottom and then reread the book, paying close attention to the information in the pictures. Even though it looks like a simple picture book, it has a lot of information."

"In *Transformed: How Everyday Things Are Made* [Slavin, 2005], it looks like each page tells about how something is created. The text is scattered in short paragraphs and captions all over the page. I'll spend a lot of time on each page, reading the text and also learning from the pictures and the sequence of steps to make each item."

"Wow! In *It's a Butterfly's Life* [Kelly, 2007], there is so much information on each page. Even though the pages are small, the author included a lot. The pictures and text are woven together so I have to make sure I don't miss anything. Some of the words go across the page but are not in a straight line. The pictures are great, so I think I'd enjoy spending lots of time on them. I'll start on the left and make sure I read one page before I go to the next."

This think-aloud session helped students see the possibilities for previewing nonfiction. After the session, Franki gave students a bit of time to preview and choose books for independent reading.

Nonfiction Mini-Lesson #3: Setting a Purpose for Nonfiction Reading

After conferring with her students, Franki realized that many of them enjoyed nonfiction, but seemed to think of it as "school reading" and therefore depended on her to set the purpose for reading it. And she wasn't surprised. As teachers, after all, we choose the texts based on curriculum content and determine what we want our students to learn from them. As such, by third grade, many students see nonfiction reading as what they must do to be successful at school.

So Franki planned another nonfiction mini-lesson reminding students about the questioning strategy they often used with fiction text. She knew that for her students to gain new information from nonfiction text, learning to note the things they were wondering as they read would help. Her students understood how to question fiction text, but they weren't doing it for nonfiction. Franki asked students to choose nonfiction books that seemed just right for them and to list three or four questions that they hoped reading the book would answer. They posted the questions on the front cover of the book to refer to as they read. For the next few days, during whole-class instruction, students shared questions that had been answered and new questions that emerged as they read. Initially Franki assumed that this strategy would naturally transfer to all reading, but it seemed that the class just needed practice.

For so many years we taught nonfiction reading skills in the content areas. This is important, but so is helping students to read nonfiction for pleasure. We have found that when we do both, reading grows.

Learning From Read-Aloud

As with every reading workshop routine, read-aloud is rich with assessment opportunities. We learn about our students by paying attention to what they do and say in read-aloud. We pay close attention to comments students make and questions that they ask. We look closely at their read-aloud notebooks to determine how they are using them to understand books. The information we gain in read-aloud gives us insight into the needs of our students. When we see patterns of confusion, we plan mini-lessons. Making evidence-based predictions and identifying themes in books are typical topics.

Making Predictions

Franki noticed early one year that her third graders enjoyed making predictions while reading fiction, based on evidence from the

> ### Simple Picture Books With Surprises
> ◆ *Hurry! Hurry!* by Eve Bunting
> ◆ *Bark, George* by Jules Feiffer
> ◆ *Grandpa's Teeth* by Rod Clement
> ◆ *Tough Boris* by Mem Fox
> ◆ *Out of the Egg* by Tina Matthews

text, and they were comfortable sharing them during the read-aloud. They were good at it, too, but they would hold on to their predictions, no matter what happened in the story. So she decided to use mini-lesson time to address the problem. Her goal was to help students let go of initial predictions when the text offered evidence that no longer supported them. She used simple picture books with surprise endings that she could read quickly. Since the pictures tell much of the story in these books, comprehending the text generally isn't an issue.

Franki began the lesson by discussing how authors put surprises in their books and that good readers know that and are prepared to change their predictions as the story unfolds.

Our students often have difficulty using comprehension strategies in longer texts. Picture books help by providing a manageable context for talking about sophisticated strategies. Once the students are comfortable with applying a strategy to picture books, they usually can carry the skill over to longer texts.

Identifying Themes

When we read novels to the class, we listen for whether our students recognize and understand themes. This can be difficult for them. Often, they can find the big idea, such as "friendship," but can't identify a specific theme. For example, while listening to *The Tale of Despereaux*, Franki's students noticed that the book was about love and sadness, but they couldn't go any deeper than that. They didn't realize that themes span the entire book. Instead, they thought themes applied to single events. So Franki gathered some picture books with accessible

> ### Picture Books With Accessible Themes
> ◆ *The Table Where Rich People Sit* by Byrd Baylor
> ◆ *The Summer My Father Was Ten* by Pat Brisson
> ◆ *The Runaway Bunny* by Margaret Wise Brown
> ◆ *Walk On: A Guide for Babies of All Ages* by Marla Frazee
> ◆ *Lost and Found* by Oliver Jeffers
> ◆ *Anthony and the Girls* by Oliver Konnecke
> ◆ *Stand Tall, Molly Lou Melton* by Patty Lovell
> ◆ *Learning to Fly* by Sebastian Meschenmoser
> ◆ *So Few of Me* by Peter Reynolds
> ◆ *The Other Side* by Jacqueline Woodson

themes for mini-lessons, knowing that if students could find themes in these books, they would be able to transfer the skill to longer books.

Over several days of mini-lessons, Franki taught the language used in talking about themes and the strategies necessary to identify themes in longer works.

Learning From Class Reflections and Assessments

As discussed earlier in the book, we gather a great deal of information from students' reflective writing and whole-class surveys, including the Developmental Reading Assessment survey. Early in the year, Franki noticed that many of her students did not identify favorite books and authors on the survey, and that it was difficult for them to decide what to read next. Since successful readers often choose future reading based on past favorites, this habit became a focus for mini-lessons. Throughout the year, Franki held conferences with students about their book choices, analyzed status-of-the-class notes, and looked at student reading logs periodically. She was eager to see the progress students had made when she re-administered the DRA survey again in January.

Book Choice

Based on the surveys, Franki was happy to see that all her students could now identify favorite books and authors and were using that skill to think ahead in their reading. She also noted that most students were now reading books in more than one genre and most were choosing books that were right for them. They were pleased with themselves when they finished a good book. They found characters they loved and could get lost in books.

However, as she looked further, she noticed that many of her students had told her that they wanted to read "fatter" and "longer" and "harder" books. This gave her pause because she knew that if students consistently read books that are too long or difficult, they will not grow as readers. She was also a little concerned about the value students were placing on these challenging books. After all, most of these third and fourth graders had just begun reading chapter books and were just gaining the necessary stamina to stick with those books.

Franki wanted to help students see that choosing just-right books is not simply a matter of length and difficulty. A reader's mood and interests, and the text's features are important as well. At the same time, she did not want to discourage students who were successful with longer novels. She wanted all students to be comfortable with where they were as readers and to use their knowledge of themselves as readers to choose great books.

So Franki planned several mini-lessons on book choice to help students see the value of a diverse reading diet. She thought about her own life as a reader. She looked at the shelf of books she had read over the last few years, focusing on the genre, topic, length, and difficulty. She wanted her students to see that all of these books (no matter how long or fat) were just right for her when she read them. She wanted to show them that she wasn't always looking for harder and fatter books in order to grow as a reader; her mood, life circumstance, and purpose for the reading had much more to do with her book choices. She brought in short books that she read when she didn't have a lot of time, long books that she saved for traveling or vacation when she had more time, books by authors she loves, and nonfiction on topics that interest her.

Our Thinking About Just-Right Books

- Previewing helps me decide whether a book is right for me.

- I have to think about my mood. Do I want an adventure? A sad book?

- I look at the size of the lettering or font.

- I usually like books with an interesting plot.

- Sometimes I need an "in-between book" between longer novels.

- I look at the way the book is set up. Is the layout easy for me to understand?

- I try to think about my tastes right now.

- I think about how long it is. Is it too long for me right now?

- I wonder if the book is one I will want to go back to and reread.

- I take recommendations from people I trust.

- I think about how much time I have to read. Do I need a light read? Do I have time to get into a long book?

- Sometimes when it is football season, I want to read a book about football or with a character who plays football.

Later that week, she followed up with another mini-lesson to expand students' ideas of just-right books. She asked students how the books they were reading at the time were just right for them. Then, together, they created a chart of characteristics that made a book just right.

Students clearly understood that just-right books aren't necessarily longer and harder. Franki built on this understanding in informal conversations and in individual conferences.

Learning From Conferences

We gather a great deal of ideas for mini-lessons from conferences. Although our main goal of conferring is to address individual student's needs, we also look for patterns that emerge that give us insight into the needs of the whole class and a focus for our mini-lessons. These teacher-led mini-lessons are built upon the conversations we have with children during individual conferences.

Determining the Meaning of Words

When students are struggling, they often aren't able to give us concrete information about what challenges them. Instead, they simply claim the book is boring or they "don't get it." In conferences, we try to get to the bottom of the issue. Recently, Franki realized that many of her students were having trouble comprehending what they were reading because of difficult vocabulary. They would read through words they could pronounce, but wouldn't stop to consider the meaning of the word. As a result, their comprehension was breaking down. Franki realized that many of the students believed that saying the word was enough, so the more important issue of word meaning became a topic for the next day's mini-lesson.

Sharing New Books

When conferring with her third and fourth graders, Franki noticed that many of them were reading books that were too difficult. At the same time, those same students were also reading books with funny characters such as Junie B. Jones and Judy Moody—books that were *not* too difficult. In a mini-lesson later that week, she shared a stack of those books, such as *Clementine* (Pennypacker, 2006) and

Books With Funny Characters
- *Skinnybones* by Barbara Park
- *Clementine* by Sara Pennypacker
- *Ivy and Bean* by Annie Barrows
- *Stink* by Megan McDonald
- *Shredderman: Secret Identity* by Wendelin Van Draanen

Ivy and Bean (Barrows, 2007), which showed the value of the easier books students were reading and introduced several humorous characters to the whole class. She demonstrated that just-right books could be books that had funny main characters.

Making Time for Student-Led Mini-Lessons

When we discover a student using a new strategy or trying a new approach that may help other students, we might ask that student to share what he or she is doing in a mini-lesson. It is very powerful for students to invite others to try a strategy or behavior that works for them. Joanne Hindley addresses this in her book *In the Company of Children* (1996) when she says, "My job is to marvel at all that unfolds before me, to recognize the strengths and needs of individual readers and to wonder about the implications of what I see for whole-class instruction" (p. 102).

We recommend student-led mini-lessons based on assessments conducted throughout the reading workshop. For example, when we are conferring with a child, we are assessing that child's strengths, but we are also thinking about how the child's strengths might be incorporated in a lesson with the entire class. When a conference helps a student become more independent, we often ask that child to share what he or she has learned in a mini-lesson. We like to invite students to lead mini-lessons because of the powerful impact it has on learning and community building.

When students share their thinking in a mini-lesson, they recognize the importance of their thinking as well as its impact on the learning of the whole class. These lessons also build reader identity since children must articulate their behaviors, skills, and strategies.

Building Stamina

One year, Brennen was reading a long chapter book called *Peter and the Shadow Thieves* (Barry & Pearson, 2006), but when he was three-quarters of the way through it, he was ready to give up. The book was dragging on. During a conference, Brennen and Franki tried to determine whether the book was worth finishing. Franki shared with Brennen a technique she used— counting the pages she has left and dividing that number by the days she has left to complete the book. This gives her a daily reading goal that feels much more manageable than one unscheduled goal for the entire book. So Brennen and Franki used a calculator and sticky notes to mark the next seven days' worth of reading. They put dates on each sticky note, reminding Brennen of the reading he should do each day. Franki's main concern was not that he finish the book, but that he had a strategy that would help him with future reading as he moved to longer and more difficult books.

At the end of the conference, Franki asked Brennen to meet with her after the seven days of reading. She asked him to think about the strategy, whether it worked for him and whether it would be worth sharing with the class. When it was time to meet, Brennen had finished the book and was eager to share the strategy with the class, hoping that it would help others who were in the same situation.

Sustaining Comprehension

In the late fall of one year, Franki held a conference with a few students who were quitting almost every book they started. When she talked with them, they said they did not like the books they were reading. They wanted to quit the books and try to find "better" books. Franki listened to students, trying to find out what was making them lose stamina.

After several conferences, Franki realized that students were quitting books because they couldn't hold a story line and a set of characters with several days between readings. Most of the students were new to chapter books, so this was a challenge. Earlier in the year in a conference, Franki had taught Maggie to keep track of her reading by writing a one-sentence summary on a sticky note and placing it where she stopped reading. Then, when she would resume reading, she could look back at the sticky notes to refresh her memory. Maggie shared this strategy as a whole-class mini-lesson, and it was helpful to many of the students who were quitting books.

Understanding Unique Features of a Book

Students often encounter unique features in the books they are reading, such as maps, author notes, and family trees, and need help navigating them. One year, William chose a book with a prologue. He requested a conference with Franki because he wasn't sure what a prologue was. He had never encountered one, and wasn't sure how it connected to the story. William and Franki worked through the prologue and discussed its purpose. When he finished the book, William met with Franki to discuss the reasons the author may have included the prologue. Later, she asked William to share his learning with the class so that others knew what to expect when they encountered a prologue.

Closing Thoughts

Whole-class instruction helps all students move forward. We have learned how to use our observations and assessments in all areas of the reading workshop to shape mini-lessons that we lead and students lead.

In the next chapter, we will discuss how we plan and orchestrate small-group instruction. We will focus on *guiding* readers toward independence, and we will share examples of student-initiated and teacher-initiated small-group instruction.

Chapter 6

Small-Group Instruction

> ❝The metaphor that has informed my vision of reading workshop, right from the start, is the dining room table–my dining room table, around which my family and friends talk easily and often about the books we're reading. I'm on a never-ending quest to get that table into my classroom...❞
>
> —Nancie Atwell, *The Reading Zone: How to Help Kids Become Skilled, Passionate, Habitual, Critical Readers (2007)*

For so long, we did not include small-group instruction in our reading workshops because it reminded us of the round-robin reading groups of our childhood, which we did not want for our students. Instead, we met with students individually in conferences. After a while, we started to notice that our conferences sounded the same from one to the next, since several students were struggling with the same challenges in their reading. It seemed silly *not* to put these students together in a group. We agree with Irene Fountas and Gay Su Pinnell when they say, "If the teacher's job is to take each child from where he is to where he needs to go in reading, then that teacher must assess individuals. With a class of twenty to thirty-five youngsters, grouping for instruction makes sense. As teachers, we want to make learning manageable yet avoid the negative aspects of grouping. We want to be sure children are working with materials that help them take the next step in learning to read" (1996, p. xv).

Now, during the 30 to 45 minutes of independent reading time, we work with individuals and small groups. If the need is specific to one child, we meet with her in a conference. If several students have similar needs, we create a small group. These groups are very different from the reading groups of our childhood in that they help us meet our students' needs and use our reading workshop time effectively.

Rethinking Guided Reading in Grades 3–6

So often in education we come across a truly original idea that assists students in their journey to becoming independent readers. In most cases, the intentions of those who come up with the idea are good, but something happens along the way. The idea becomes institutionalized, and managing it becomes more important than teaching students. We lose our focus on individual students. In our estimation, guided reading falls into that category.

We believe in the principles of guided reading—the fact that it ensures that students are taught in groups with others who have similar needs. It makes sense to look for patterns of need and to group students accordingly.

However, over time, we realized that managing guided-reading groups actually *limited* our ability to teach. Instead of looking at daily assessments and determining how best to meet each child's needs, we were getting caught up in the number of groups we scheduled each day, the number of students in each group, the length of time each group met, and the text level of the students in the group. Our reading workshop turned into a stressful push to make guided-reading groups work instead of meeting the needs of readers. Cathy Mere, author of *More Than Guided Reading: Finding the Right Instructional Mix, K-3,* says, "My teaching had become so focused on guided reading that my vision of what was possible had narrowed. Guided reading had provided a structure for reading instruction and had helped me to learn to identify what students needed, but it had not helped students to connect this learning to their reading lives" (2005, p. 8).

In recent years, we've changed the way we think about small groups. Instead of managing guided-reading groups, we *guide readers* (Mere, 2005). Instead of relying on structures that define and limit our teaching, we initiate routines that give us endless opportunities to teach and assess as our students participate in a literature-rich reading community. Everything we understand about the readers in our classroom informs our small-group instruction, which moves students toward independence.

When we are guiding readers, we honor what they know, build on their strengths, and help them realize their unlimited potential. When we are guiding readers, we respect them as thinkers and problem solvers, involve them in the grouping process, and make wise decisions in our planning and teaching. We guide readers toward independence based on the following considerations:

- What we know about our students
- What their goals are for their reading
- What our goals and expectations are for them as readers
- What we learn about them as readers from our assessments
- What standards we want to teach
- What routines we design for our classroom
- How we design our classroom space and allocate reading time
- The big messages we want our students to get from our teaching

Guiding readers is not restricted to small-group instruction. We guide readers during every routine. In whole-class lessons, we talk about what good readers do, practice strategies that help students make sense of texts, and help them understand themselves as readers. Read-aloud time is a critical whole-class routine in which we model what successful readers do and promote reading as thinking. Small-group instruction is just one more way in which we guide readers and give them the support they need to become independent.

Orchestrating Small-Group Instruction

Because our goal for reading workshop is to guide readers to independence, we orchestrate small-group instruction to meet that goal. That means we don't meet with equal-sized groups all the time, on certain days of the week. We don't require every child to participate in a small group every week. Instead of having students read the same book at a kidney-shaped table, our students read a variety of books in a variety of places around the classroom.

In small-group lessons, we use short texts to guide readers in skills and strategies without investing a lot of time on a novel or lengthy informational text. We can complete lessons in a relatively short time and send students off to use the strategy in their independent reading.

In small groups, we rely less on reading texts at the right levels and more on learning a variety of strategies. Students may all read a short article and practice a strategy, or they may come with books they are reading during independent reading time and learn a new strategy. There is no set format, in other words. Honest conversations prevail, as readers talk about what is hard or easy for them. Sometimes the conversations are about how their thinking changes as they make their way through a text. Above all, as we guide readers, we encourage them to take risks in their reading, thinking, and talking.

Small-group instruction is a fluid process. It is not a structure to be followed, but a foundation for deeper thinking. Guiding readers relies on listening to children, watching them as they read and talk to one another, and collecting evidence of their learning. It assumes we are always learning to read and that we can learn from each other. For the teacher, it means reflecting on what students need and how to most effectively engage them in authentic reading experiences.

Creating Spaces for Small-Group Instruction

Before school begins in the fall, we create spaces that invite small-group work. Rather than one central meeting spot, we create several places that are directly tied to the size of the group and the goal of the lesson. Some groups may be made up of only two students, others may have six or more. Because of these variations in size, it is important that we are flexible in using classroom space.

Choosing a space that is comfortable for students and supports whatever is being taught is important. Franki has a dining room table in her classroom that is a great space to meet with four to six students because it invites casual conversation. She also has a small coffee table that is great for groups of two to six. Franki uses this table when she wants to gather information informally or have introductory conversations. Franki has also created a space on the floor near the easel, which is perfect for explicit teaching. Having many places for groups to meet encourages small-group learning and teaching.

We no longer have kidney-shaped tables in our classrooms because they don't support quality talk and empower students. When the teacher sits on one side of the table with the children on the other, the teacher is in charge. It is important for everyone to have equal membership in the group and to be comfortable sharing their thinking with one another.

We created a space near the easel for some small-group work.

We meet with students in a circle on the floor.

Day-to-Day Assessment in the Reading Workshop

Our classroom has different-size tables to accommodate different-size groups.

A coffee table provides a casual place for small groups.

Student-Initiated Groups

When students are given the opportunity to talk about themselves as readers, they develop a clear understanding of their needs as readers. When we form groups, we want students to know they have a stake in their learning. We want students to recognize that when they work in small groups, they can accomplish more than they can working on their own.

When we involve students in planning for small groups, we ask them to fill out a reflection sheet listing their strengths and goals. We also include a question that asks them to identify those goals that might best be met in small-group work. Based on these assessments, we often discover that students are unsure of concepts and strategies that we thought they had mastered. We combine our knowledge of them as readers with their own knowledge to identify a focus for small groups.

Name _Shivani_   Date _10/2_

Which Reading Workshop group/groups did you sign up for?

1. Stick with one book

2. try more challenging books

3. reading aloud more fluently

Why did you decide to sign up for each group?

1. I decided to sign up for the sticking with one book until I'm finished because sometimes I have two book going on at the same time and it confuses me.

How do you hope these groups will help you as a reader?

I think these groups will help me as a reader because it might help me set more goals as a reader

Do you have any other reading goals?

I do not have any.

Two different forms that we use to help students think about how small groups can help them meet their goals.

Name _Sydney_   Date _12/7/_

Thinking Ahead in Reading

What are the 3 things that will help you the most as a reader?
Which skills/strategies do you need to become an even better reader?

1. understanding poetry that don't ryme.
2. Nonfiction reading understanding.
3. figureing out the theme.

Which of the skills do you think is the most important for you right now? Why do you think so? Be specific.

understanding Nonfiction reading.
Because we are reading alot of it
rite now and reading for our progects
to understand it for papers and
stuff.

How might a group help you with each of these goals? What are you hoping to gain from a group focusing on these skills/strategies?

1. I think a group would help because
we could read them and understand them
together. make stageis to help. likeing
poetry more because are age is more
of not ryming. reading it more.
couldn't really help you mabe give
you some stradageis. because
you need to think on your
own.

3. for a read aloud book we could
think of a theme and come out
knowing how to find the theme.

After students have completed the reflection sheet, we follow up with a whole-class conversation. We ask students to think about the goals they need help reaching and those they can reach on their own. For example, a student whose goal is to read more books by a particular author can accomplish this on his own. A student who wants to read more nonfiction may need the support of others who are doing the same thing. The same is true of students who want to work on figuring out unknown words. Because of these whole-class conversations, students begin to feel comfortable talking about their strengths and weaknesses as readers and recognizing that sometimes we all need support to grow as readers.

We finish the conversation by brainstorming with the class a list of possible topics for small groups. We create sign-up sheets, inviting students to join a group over the next few days. If more than ten students sign up for a group, we either split the group into smaller groups to promote conversation or consider the topic for whole-class lessons.

A student signs up for small groups.

We review the sign-up sheets and consider what we know about each student. Then we make instructional plans for how often each group might meet, whether they need a common text or a variety of texts. We make sure everyone has signed up for at least one group. (We usually tell students they must sign up for at least one and no more than three.) We check to see if students would benefit from groups that they did not sign up for and consider inviting them to join. We take note of students who sign up for groups that we didn't realize they needed. All of these observations contribute to the class profile we create through assessment.

Once these groups are established, we take the lead. We look back at assessments related to each individual in the group, meet with the group, and get students started in their work.

A Group on Fluency

One year, while discussing their goals, many of Franki's students expressed a desire to be more comfortable reading aloud, so Franki created a sign-up sheet for a small group. During the meeting, Franki started off, as she often does, asking students why they had signed up for the group. As they spoke, Franki took notes and noticed a pattern. Many students claimed they had trouble pronouncing words, which forced them to pause frequently when reading aloud.

These students needed to devote time to fluency, so Franki sent them each off with a stack of sticky notes to mark in their books places where they noticed their fluency was breaking down and to underline words that got in the way of their fluency. She then asked them to copy onto a chart the sentences containing those words. Franki would look at those sentences for patterns and determine the types of words that were keeping them from reading fluently.

Over the next few days, the chart grew as students added sentences. Franki noticed a clear pattern of students being stumped by words of three syllables or more. Her work with this group would focus on ways to figure out unknown words from their context.

A student adds a sentence to the fluency group's chart.

Franki could have had these students practice reading simple text repeatedly, or perform rs Theater, but that probably wouldn't have helped them. These students could not read fluently because they did not have the skills to decode multisyllabic words. The first group meeting provided a setting to assess exactly what was getting in the way of their fluency.

A Group on Reading Stamina

Another group came together, made up largely of students who were new to chapter books, to work on sticking with a book to the end. Although all members were quitting most books that they started, each student seemed to quit at different points and for different reasons. When Franki looked at the list of students who had signed up for this group, she referred to the status-of-the-class sheet to see the kinds of reading these students had been doing. A few students were choosing books that were too hard, one student was choosing books that were just right but was not previewing them, while others were choosing books that simply didn't engage them.

Franki could not teach one skill to address every need of the students in the group, so she decided to teach a few. She knew that better previewing skills would help, as well as skills in setting daily goals and using sticky notes to summarize daily reading. It was tempting to just assign this group one book and guide them through the reading of it. However, if Franki did that, students would probably finish that book without developing new skills for completing future books. So Franki met with this group several times over the next few weeks to help them monitor themselves, and to give them stamina-building strategies, such as talking to others who have loved the book when you get to a boring spot and want to quit.

For the first group lesson, Franki had students bring a stack of books they were thinking of reading next. She led students through a good preview of each book. Once group members chose a book to read, Franki asked them to mark places with sticky notes where they found themselves wanting to quit. Then they met a second time to share and compare the reasons they wanted to quit.

For the third small-group lesson, Franki invited students who were successful at finishing books to share their strategies. Some of these students had conferred with Franki about quitting books in the past, so they could speak wisely from experience. Here are some of their words of advice:

- Talk to someone about it
- Use sticky notes to write summaries of the chapter and then reread all of those before starting to read each day
- Read the front flap and the table of contents each day before reading
- Read the boring part out loud to someone until it isn't boring anymore

Before the final lesson, Franki asked students to try these strategies and be prepared to talk about those that worked for them. She followed up over the next several weeks with individual conferences, reminding students of the strategies. She continued to monitor their reading and assess their ability to transfer strategies to other texts.

Name **Madeline**

Sticking With a Book

Book Title	Date	Easy or Hard?	Why?
Dragon Rider	11-9-06	Easy	Because I got exited on chapter eight-teen and read it.
Dragon Rider	11-10-06	Easy	Because I got a little bit of reading in.
Dragon Rider	11-15-06	Easy	Because I got 2 chapters read.
Dragon Rider	11-17-06	Easy	Because I got a lot of my book read.
Dragon Rider	11-27-06	Easy	I got a lot of reading in.

Students monitored how difficult it was to stick with a book they had committed to.

Teacher-Initiated, Teacher-Led Groups

When student-initiated groups do not address all that we know students need based on our assessments and expectations, we step in and initiate and lead groups. When we plan these groups, we think about the learning that is happening in read-aloud, mini-lessons, and conferences. The form on page 132 (Sibberson & Szymusiak, 2003) helps us think through the planning of small-group instruction, as well as other routines of the reading workshop.

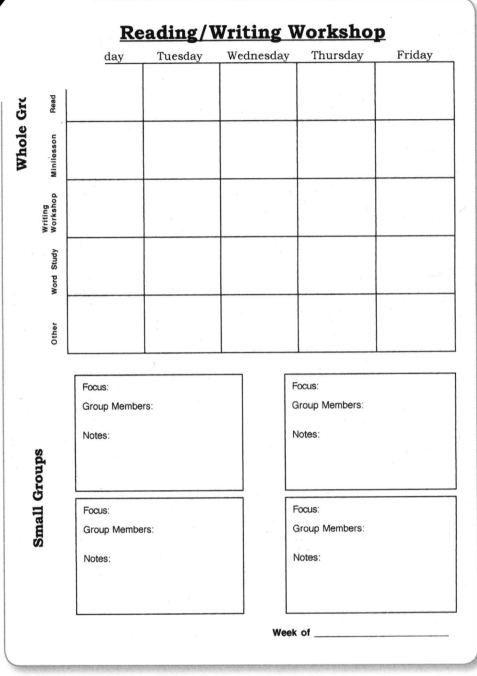

Reading/Writing Workshop

		...day	Tuesday	Wednesday	Thursday	Friday
Whole Group	Read					
	Minilesson					
	Writing Workshop					
	Word Study					
	Other					

Small Groups

Focus:

Group Members:

Notes:

Focus:

Group Members:

Notes:

Focus:

Group Members:

Notes:

Focus:

Group Members:

Notes:

Week of _____

We use this form to think through whole-class and small-group instruction.

A Group on Written Retellings

We know that retelling or summarizing a text in one's own words builds comprehension. To develop this skill, we ask students to give oral retellings of books we've read aloud. Eventually, they become skillful at written retellings of books they've read independently. Franki noticed that John and Kelly were having difficulty with retellings, so she met with each of them in a conference and asked them to retell the chapter they were reading. Not surprisingly, they had no trouble retelling orally, but their written retellings lacked clarity and completeness. These students were comprehending the text just fine, but they could not transfer their oral retellings to writing. So Franki shared a graphic organizer from *Tell Me a Story: Developmentally Appropriate Retelling Strategies* (Hansen, 2004) that helps students organize their thinking before writing. Since both students struggled a bit with writing in general, she knew practice like this would help them. By helping John and Kelly plan out their retellings, Franki ensured they didn't skip parts of the story they knew were important.

A Group on the Value of Rereading

One year, Franki's students were talking during read-aloud about *Loser* (Spinelli, 2003), the book she was going to read aloud next. Some students complained that they had read the book before. Franki said, "Oh, good, you'll be able to read it so differently since you know the plot. Is there anyone else who has already read the book? Let's meet in a small group during reading workshop to come up with ideas about how you might think about the book differently this time through."

In the group, Franki helped the students see that a second reading can help us dig deeper and notice things we hadn't noticed the first time. She met with this group periodically throughout the read-aloud so students could talk about the things they were noticing, without giving away the plot to the whole class.

Regardless of who initiates the group, students are always welcome to join in a group that seems worthwhile. When we initiate a group, we invite the students who we want to be part of it. Then we ask if anyone else wants to join. This way, students become very honest about their needs and happy to join groups that can help them.

Teacher-Initiated, Student-Led Groups

Sometimes our students share a strategy or skill in a conference that we know would benefit many other students. For example, when Maria was reading A Series of Unfortunate Events by Lemony Snicket, she realized that the character named Sunny was always happy and cheerful. She wondered if the author had named her purposely and decided to track the other characters' names in a notebook to find out. Each time a new character was introduced, she would add the name and its definition to her notebook. When Maria looked up *Olaf*, the name of the antagonist in the story, she found out that it meant "ancestor." Maria discovered that all the names had a meaning that helped her understand each character better. She was excited about this discovery.

Because so many other students enjoyed this series, Franki asked Maria to share her discoveries with a small group. The others were excited to think in a new way about this beloved series. Some shared their own discoveries, and Maria's idea snowballed. For example, while reading *Kira-Kira* (Kadohata, 2004) during independent reading time, wherever a new character was introduced, Mei looked up the definition of the character's name, wrote it on a sticky note, and placed the note on the page. That way, as she was reading, she could look back and remind herself of each character by reading her note *and* the author's introduction of the character.

Voluntary Book Clubs

Once children are comfortable discussing books in small groups, they are ready for voluntary, small-group book clubs, which give them the chance to talk to peers about a book they have read, and think deeply about it. We try to be authentic about all areas of reading instruction, so we keep these book talks as authentic as they would be outside of a school setting.

A few years ago, Franki invited adults who participate in book clubs to come in and talk to the class each day for a week or two. The class learned so many things from the experience. These are the main things they learned about book clubs:

- Most people choose a book club because they like the people in the group.
- Members of book clubs pick books in different ways.
- Some clubs allow the person hosting to choose a book; some negotiate the whole year's worth of books in advance; others always read a book by an author members love.
- Most book clubs talk about the book only when everyone has finished it.
- Sometimes people in book clubs don't finish the book.
- Some people are in one book club per month. Others part in or four clubs a month.

> Dear MrsSibberson,
>
> I am really really excited about the book groups. I think it will be interesting to see just what everyone else thinks of the book. I wonder if it will be the same as the mother daughter book discussion?
>
> I like Mrs. Moreghans idea of reading a book around 200 pages long. I also like the idea of dif authors. Will this be one group the whole time for book discussions or will we be switching groups every time?
>
> I have some book recomendations:
> Small Steps - This was a book for my book group. I think it is a good book to talk about because it is an autobiography and you can really talk about how she felt and connections ect
> Among the hidden - great plot, Interesting plot, confusing plot.
> Angelfish - This book had intresting but confusing characters. It has a very interesting mix of characters also. And it is sometimes funny or serious. It also has an interesting Plot.

Students wrote letters to Franki about their interests in book clubs.

Before starting book clubs that year, Franki's class talked about the way they might work. Franki then had students write letters to her about their thoughts on book clubs, in which they answered questions about their level of excitement about book clubs and whether they had suggestions for books to read and discuss. (See example on the previous page.) These conversations and letters helped Franki to assess where the students were in their thinking before book clubs began. She learned that students already had ideas about the books they wanted to read and discuss. She learned that, like adults, all of the students wanted to choose their own groups. She learned that some students wanted to be in several book clubs while others wanted to protect their independent reading time, and only wanted to be in one group. Those students met in their book clubs for the few times it took to talk about the chosen book, but during the rest of the quarter, they would be dedicated to their own independent reading time. Together the class made a few rules for clubs:

- Everyone has to be in at least one book club for the nine weeks. Students could be in multiple clubs through the course of the quarter.

- No one can exclude anyone from a book club.

- The club can meet after finishing the book or while still reading it.

- Since some students would join multiple book clubs, the clubs meet at scheduled times, which are marked on the class calendar so they don't overlap with any other groups scheduled during reading workshop.

Franki created a space on a large bulletin board for book club sign-up sheets. To get things started, she chose the initial books—books that she loved. Interestingly, no one signed up for these book clubs. Instead, over the next few days, the board filled with sign-up sheets for book clubs based on good books that students had selected. Over the next few weeks, groups set dates, met to discuss books, and signed up for more clubs. Book club soon became

Small groups and book clubs are scheduled on a classroom calendar. This is what a calendar looks like at the start of the year. It will be filled in as the months progress.

part of the fabric of the workshop—one more opportunity for the students to grow as readers.

Once talks got underway, Franki made a point to keep her distance. She had discovered long ago that her participation in student-initiated groups often stifled the conversation. So, she sat across the room, watching and listening. Other times she would join the group, but sit behind students so that it was clear that she was just there to observe. She didn't get caught up in whether students understood the book. She didn't jump in to correct their thinking. Instead, she thought through the things that she wanted to learn from students, only dropping questions occasionally to encourage them to go deeper in their discussion of the book.

Questions Franki Might Ask as She Listens In on Book Clubs

- What made you think that?
- Have you thought about the title?
- How are you using your notes to think hard about one issue?
- Have you talked about characters yet?
- Have you thought about recording your thinking—do you need any tools from me?

Assessing in Book Clubs

When we think about what we want students to get out of book clubs, we focus on process—things that will help them read and think about text differently the next time they pick up a book. As the clubs progress throughout the year, the responses become deeper. The unique ways in which students respond provide a great deal of information for us.

What Franki Might Notice When She Listens In on Book Clubs

- Using a new strategy to track changes in a character
- Making predictions with little or no evidence to support them
- Building on each other's thinking
- Taking turns round-robin style, without building on thinking
- Finding a way to decide what is most important to discuss

Students find a variety of ways to record their thinking in book clubs.

Robinson Crusoe
SCHOLASTIC Treasury

ch 1. I'm saved from the sea
ch 2. I get back to the ship
ch 3. I make many trips to the ship
ch 4. Building a home
ch 5. Making the things I need.
ch 6. Getting food
ch 7. The years past by
ch 8. A change in my life
ch 9. Cannibals
ch 10. Friday
ch 11. My life with friday
ch 12. I teach Friday
ch 13. A Rescue

ch 1. How I left Home
ch 2. My Adventures with the p
ch 3. I become a castaway
ch 4. Rescuing Valuable item
ch 5. I build a Shelter a food.
ch 6. A terrible illness
ch 7. I Adapt to island li
ch 8. I try to escape by boa
ch 9. A footprint in the Sa
ch 10. Cannibals visit my i
ch 11. Another shipwreck

Maniac Magee
Life Issues

Blacks and whites being together — He made them feel different about each other. He brought them together

Bravness He did what people told him to do and at his own ratcatc was brave and did not care what side he was on

Confidence he was confident in his self that he was und the not confident for what he belived in

* Not having a home He didn't care that he did not have a home and he did not want to go with amanda

Family ←

Friendship — He made friends and made people make friends. He kept his friends by not bragging and not being selfish.

Day-to-Day Assessment in the Reading Workshop

Our students' responses served a number of purposes. They provided us with information about how students were thinking about text. They provided us with great ideas for mini-lessons. And each time a group tried something new, one more tool became available for the rest of the class to try. Our role was to help facilitate the spreading of ideas.

When Hillary's group tracked the ways in which characters changed over the course of *Takeoffs and Landings* (Haddix, 2003), Franki asked the group to talk about this strategy in a mini-lesson. When Alex's group compared two abridged versions of *Robinson Crusoe* on a large chart, Franki asked that group to share as well. Franki is always providing new ways for students to respond to books.

The reflection sheet that students fill out following a book club is an especially useful assessment tool because it gives us information about students' experiences. It tells us how they used their skills and strategies and what they got out of the conversation. In addition to assigning reflection sheets, Franki observed, watching to see how each student participated and how the group's thinking grew.

Plan for Reading Discussion Group

What book/piece will you be reading and discussing with your group?

How did you decide on this book?

Why does this book/piece interest you?

Why do you think the book is talkworthy?

List the members of your group?

When will your group meet?

How will you prepare for the discussion?

Before the Discussion

How did you prepare for your book club?

What are some things you'd like to discuss?

After the Discussion

What was the most important thing discussed? Why was it interesting or important?

Did someone in the group say something that changed or added to your original thinking about the book? Describe it.

Did someone share something that was new thinking for you—something you had not thought about on your own? Explain.

How did participating in this book talk add to what you know about books and reading?

Students fill out reflection sheets like these as part of their book club experience. They help us assess these groups without sitting in on every conversation.

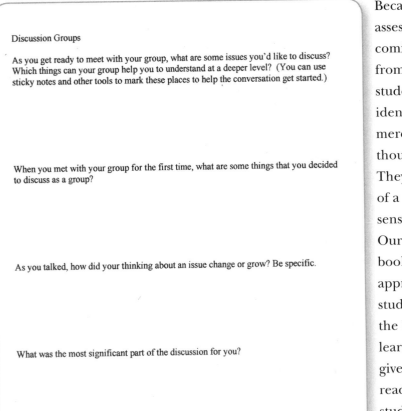

Discussion Groups

As you get ready to meet with your group, what are some issues you'd like to discuss? Which things can your group help you to understand at a deeper level? (You can use sticky notes and other tools to mark these places to help the conversation get started.)

When you met with your group for the first time, what are some things that you decided to discuss as a group?

As you talked, how did your thinking about an issue change or grow? Be specific.

What was the most significant part of the discussion for you?

How did participating in a group help you as a reader?

Because she was carrying out these assessments, Franki was comfortable distancing herself from the groups. As a result, students could build their own identities as readers. They didn't merely respond in ways they thought she would approve of. They responded honestly, as part of a peer group, to make better sense of a variety of texts.

Our hope is that talking about books will change the way students approach their reading. We want students to see the possibilities in the books that they read. All they learn about the ways books work gives them a new tool for future reading. So we listen to make sure students are having conversations that will help them in the long run. We also listen for evidence of things that may have been planted in earlier book clubs.

When Carrie's group was discussing Neil Gaiman's *Coraline* (2006), they sorted the sticky notes into categories, then realized that they had each marked places in the text that talked about the cat, "the other mother," and the main character. Putting their sticky notes in categories helped them to focus their talk. Just as we find one topic to build on during read-aloud, this group decided to do the same in their book group.

When discussing *Touching Spirit Bear* (Mikaelsen, 2001) students paid close attention to the blanket that comes up throughout the book. They remembered that things that come up over and over in a book often have special importance. So their talk revolved around the blanket.

Sometimes book club conversations go wrong. Students might have a major misunderstanding about the book. They might focus on a topic that isn't taking them anywhere. They might not be working together to build on one another's ideas. We try hard not to interfere by "correcting" students because we don't want to take the ownership of what they read away from them or give them the message that they can't solve problems on their own. So we have to be careful with our questions and comments. We have to remember our goal is for them to learn how to talk about books, not necessarily to figure out one particular book.

Franki was listening in on a book club that was discussing *The Lion, the Witch and the Wardrobe* (Lewis, 1950). The predictions that students were making were not at all supported by the text. Instead of "fixing" their thinking, Franki asked the group to consider clues the author had given them. Then she suggested that they go back and reread to find evidence for their predictions. Doing so helped them make better-informed predictions.

Just as with more explicit small-group instruction, we make sure everyone benefits from what is learned in book clubs. When one group tracked evidence in *So B. It* (Weeks, 2004) to figure out what the title meant, Franki saw this as a new possibility for deeper reading that other students might want to try. She invites groups to share the things that she thinks will help others. In this way, everyone can grow from one another's experiences.

It has become clear to us over the years that as children become skilled at talking about books, the way they think about books changes. They expect depth in the text. In a fifth-grade class for example, a group of girls was meeting to plan their discussion of *Replay* (Creech, 2007). Franki thought that the group was setting dates and agreeing to the number of pages to read. Instead, she found it was meeting to share thoughts after individually previewing the text. By talking to one another about what they might expect from the book, they could agree on things they would think about while reading. They approached the book in a way that would invite deep thinking.

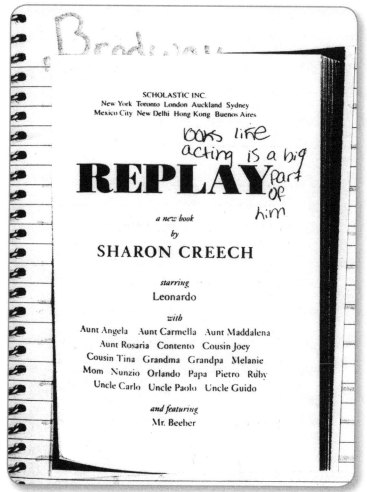

Students in the book club devoted to *Replay* by Sharon Creech met to preview the book together. Then they determined what to focus on when they read. Megan kept this club notebook to help her track these things as she read.

Clippings that might be important

Sure, his big, noisy family makes him
feel like a sardine squashed in a tin

... but in   his fantasy he gets all the attention he wants.

res, his papa seems sad and distracted ...
but Leo imagines him as a boy, tap-dancing
and singing with delight.

That's why they call Leo "fog boy." He's
always dreaming, always replaying things in
his brain. He fantasizes about who he is in
order to discover who he will become. But in the
play that is his life, Leo is eager to discover
what part will be his.

Inside Information

Mr. Beebers play: RumPoPos Porch
Why is melenie so "dredful?"

Why does he think the aunts are:
Pouty, Perfect, nosy, and invisible

Annoying Tina and joey, How are
they annoying.
Why is uncle Guido a Peace
maker. why is uncle Carlo called
traviling Carlo?

Why is his mom+dad frazzled?

Leos "Moody" older sister, what's so moody about her.

Why is he telling so much about
them, Is it like a acter on a
stage when they tell things about them
in intervieus and stuff.

The word Replay

Page		Sentince
1	12	1
2	13	2
3	14	3
4	15	4
5	16	5
6	17	6
7	18	7
8	19	8
9	20	9
10	21	10
11	22	11
13	14	12

Replay

questions	Predictions

Thoughts
all the worlds a stage, what part
will you play? (capter)

does he have a dream?

what it is

How it Started

He may have been given a bit part in the school play . . . but Leo dreams he is the est star on Broadway.

what does this

Leo's papa stood in the doorway, gazing down at him. "Leo, you make gold from pebbles," and the way he said it, Leo could tell that this was a good thing. **go with**

Pages	Broadway
1	1
2	2
3	3
4	4
5	5
	6

Sardines (over)

Page	Sentince

Each of these book clubs gave us an understanding about where to go next with students. We look to see which skills and strategies come naturally and which come as a challenge for the class as a whole. We also look for ways individual students respond to books. Some students are still working to keep track of the plot. Some are better able to think beyond the plot by analyzing characters and identifying themes. Does a majority of students need more practice finding evidence in the text to support their thinking? Can most of them build on each other's conversations? How can we support their deeper reading? We use these questions to monitor our students' progress in how they think about books. We go back to our original goals and give children time to practice the strategies with different texts until they are comfortable and successful using those strategies and their talk becomes more natural. Usually, within three weeks, students have many tools to help them discuss books in ways that stretch their thinking.

It's important to remember that students not only learn to talk about books in book clubs, they also learn to talk about them in read-aloud and mini-lessons. So we must look for evidence of growth in these routines as well.

Concluding Thoughts

Small-group instruction, facilitated by the teacher or the students, is a powerful routine of the reading workshop. It is a time for us to meet the needs of students, while also helping them see the power in thinking together. In the next chapter, we focus on conferring with students individually, in both formal and informal ways.

Chapter 7

Individual Reading Conferences and Share Time

> ❝Individual conferences are essential because they help the teacher make wise decisions about all other aspects of her reading instruction. In other words, what a teacher learns by conferring with students informs her read-alouds, shared readings, guided readings, and so on.❞
>
> —Shelley Harwayne, *Lifetime Guarantees: Toward Ambitious Literacy Teaching (2000)*

"Mrs. Sibberson, I thought Nancy Drew was a kid, but it said that she drives a car and that she went to the bank. Is she a grown-up?" Maty approached Franki with this question during independent reading time. The Nancy Drew book was the first mystery she'd ever read and, clearly, she was confused about the main character and needed help before continuing. So Franki provided that help.

Quick conferences like these come up often in reading workshop. These conferences, no matter the length, are critical because they provide students with needed support and strategies, and they give us the best opportunity to find out specific information about students. Even though we have been assessing during all reading workshop routines, time alone with a child allows us to focus in on skills that we want to assess, which is key to moving students forward in their reading. To each conference, we bring all we know about a child, as well as what we know about our state's standards, and continue to build a profile of him or her as a reader.

Work in small groups and in conferences often overlaps and extends from one to the other. A small group might meet about a topic, and then the same topic might come up during a student conference, or we may extend a conference to help a small group of students. What we do with students in small-group instruction and conferences is usually the same. The only real difference is the number of students we are working with at a time.

We also try to make conferences informal extensions of conversations that occur throughout the reading workshop. Many of the routines, such as the status of the class, which is described in detail on page 53, help us decide which students might benefit from a conference. We are very intentional when we talk to students; we want them to know that we are there to support them continuously.

The majority of our conferences occur during independent reading time. Sometimes we join the students wherever they happen to be reading. At other times, we ask them to sit with us at a table. We are honest with students about the reasons we want to meet with them, and they are honest with us about their hopes and challenges. Students also initiate conferences.

We don't schedule conferences weeks in advance, because we want to be responsive to our students' needs as they come up. We establish time for a few scheduled conferences each day and leave extra time for conversations we cannot anticipate. If a student is ready to quit a book and needs to be reminded of a strategy that might help her, she can't wait a week until we have time to fit her into our schedule. Also, if we fill up all of our independent reading time with conferences, we won't be able to take advantage of the day-to-day opportunities to assess children effectively.

Goals for Conferences

In every conference we aim to learn something about the child *and* to give him a tool to comprehend both the text he is reading *and* future texts. Instead of imposing our thinking on him, we empower him to work through challenges on his own. We learn more about the child and teach strategies that will build independence. Rereading when confused, using chapter titles to make educated predictions, and breaking up multisyllabic words to figure out what they mean are all strategies that help students make sense of many texts.

Questions We Typically Ask in Conferences

The questions we ask serve as invitations for students to think differently about their reading. We urge students to pay attention to their processes as readers to help them become more independent in their reading and provide us with valuable assessment data.

- Is this author new to you or have you read a book by him or her before?
- How did you hear about this book?
- This is a different kind of book for you. What made you choose it?
- Katie also read that book. Do you want to talk to her about it?
- You seem to love this book. Will you tell others about it?
- I noticed that you quit the book that you were reading. What made you decide to do that? Do you think you'll go back to it later?
- I thought there were some slow parts in that book. Did you think so? What did you do when you got to those parts?
- I hear that this book is getting great reviews. Could you let me know what you think when you are finished?
- Oh, that book is written in journal form, isn't it? Are you doing anything differently since you've never read a book written in that form before?
- At what point did you become confused? What did you do to try to help yourself?
- The writing on your sticky notes look interesting. How are you using sticky notes to help you understand the book?
- What will you read next?

Types of Conferences

In our conferences, we are always responsive to the needs of our students. In this section we will explore several different types of conferences—focusing on comprehension, text features, fluency, vocabulary, theme, characters, and nonfiction—to give an idea of the range of topics and strategies that can be addressed.

Conferences on Comprehension

We initiate many conferences because students are having difficulty comprehending the text. Sharing strategies helps them become more independent at constructing meaning. For example, when Sruti was about 60 pages into *Princess Academy* (Hale, 2006), she told Franki that she was confused about the plot.

The author continued to refer to an earlier event in the story, and Sruti couldn't remember why it was important. Franki could have worked with Sruti to find the event and tell her its significance. She could have suggested that Sruti find a new book since she was struggling with comprehension. Or she could have given Sruti a strategy that might help her.

Franki chose the last option. She told Sruti that readers often have to go back and reread to clarify a point. She suggested that it might be worthwhile for her to go back, read those first 60 pages over, and try to find the pieces that she had missed. Sruti was excited to do that, so she and Franki met again three days later, after Sruti had used the strategy to clear up her confusion. Sruti later shared the rereading strategy with the entire class in a mini-lesson.

This example represents how powerful conferences can be. Franki gave Sruti a strategy that helped her understand *Princess Academy*—her immediate need. She also introduced Sruti to a strategy she could use independently in future reading. Sruti also gained confidence because Franki gave her the opportunity to fix the problem on her own, with support. Sruti also became the class expert on rereading for understanding. Franki learned several things about Sruti in this conference:

- Sruti was aware that she was confused and needed assistance.
- She learned a strategy to help her stick with a more challenging book.
- She enthusiastically tried the strategy, which showed a level of confidence and commitment.
- She could articulate to the class how and why the strategy deepened her comprehension.

During this conference, Franki had Ohio's standard on comprehension in mind, as well as all that she knew about Sruti as a reader. She was able to gain information, teach to Sruti's immediate need, and introduce her to a strategy that she could use independently with that book and future books.

Conferences on Text Features

If we know that a student is reading a book in a format or genre that is new to her, we might call her over for a conference. For example, Allie announced in status of the class that she had decided to read *Trial by Journal* (Klise, 2001), a book that combines journal entries, newspaper articles, court documents, and other forms of authentic writing to create a story. This was a new format for Allie, and Franki wanted to assess how she was making sense of the text. Since Franki had read the book, she could talk to Allie about the plot and see whether this new format was getting in her way. She called Allie to a conference and found out that Allie had been successfully transferring strategies that she had used to read other books to this one. She was doing a great deal of rereading and using sticky notes to keep track of the new information. Franki recognized that Allie had internalized strategies that had worked previously for her and could transfer those strategies to a whole new format.

Conferences on Fluency

The Developmental Reading Assessment contains a formal fluency assessment, so we use informal fluency conferences to check in with students to see if they are making progress.

When we are interested in checking a student's fluency, we ask him to come to a conference with the book that he is reading and to read aloud from it. Beforehand, we make a photocopy of the passage he plans to read so we can follow along and mark his reading, as if we were taking a running record. Specifically, we mark the student's rereads, errors, and self-corrections on the page and keep it in the student's file. We also record pauses, phrasing, intonation, and attention to punctuation, when appropriate.

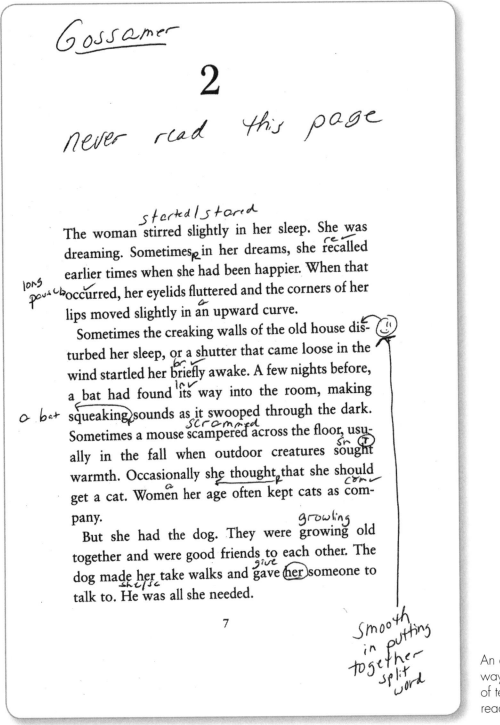

An example of the way we mark a page of text as a student reads it aloud.

Day-to-Day Assessment in the Reading Workshop

Franki takes a running record while a student reads aloud.

Also we follow up on fluency groups by meeting with students individually over the next few weeks to see how the strategies are working. For example, Franki met with students from the fluency group described on page 129 to find out if breaking up multisyllabic words was working for them in their independent reading.

Conferences on Vocabulary

Sharon had been reading *The Doll People* (Martin, 2000) for a few days, which Franki knew was the first fantasy book that Sharon had read that year. Franki also knew that the genre contains unusual vocabulary that often causes confusion among students. In the story, dolls come to life and have adventures all around a house when the humans aren't there. When humans are present, the dolls go into "doll state," a state of stillness. In a conference, Sharon told Franki she was confused about the doll state. She wondered if it was a place like Ohio State. Sharon was using what she knew to help her figure out what she didn't know, a good strategy, but it wasn't helping her. Instead of just fixing Sharon's misunderstanding, Franki had her go back and mark all of the places in the book where *doll state* was mentioned. They met again the next day to reread those places and figure out together the meaning of *doll state*. Franki supported Sharon by strengthening her understanding and showing her a strategy that could help her in future reading.

Many students' misunderstandings are at the word level. Individual words prohibit them from comprehending the text fully. Roger was just such a student. When Franki looked back at her notes, she realized that all of the times he came to her for assistance were due to unknown words in his reading. It seemed that every time he came to an unknown word, he ran for help. This pattern concerned Franki.

She started paying attention to the words that Roger struggled with across several days. She noticed that Roger could pronounce all of the words, but couldn't define them. His problem wasn't related to decoding. Franki decided that having strategies to use when he came to an unknown word could help. She worked with him on a few of the words to show him that he could figure out the gist of a sentence without knowing exactly what the one word meant. Learning to identify words that are crucial to comprehension and those that aren't helped Roger gain some independence in his reading. Franki knew that down the road, Roger would need more vocabulary work. But for now, he could use this strategy and be more engaged and confident.

Conferences on Theme

A big part of the conversation during read-aloud is thinking through the book's central theme. (See Chapter 4 for more on read-aloud.) With support, most students become skilled at recognizing and talking about possible themes, such as following your dreams in *The Invention of Hugo Cabret* (Selznick, 2007) or being true to who you are in *How to Steal a Dog* (O'Connor, 2007). However, Julie had difficulty. Her ideas always seemed a bit off, focused on a small message rather than a big theme. Realizing this helped Franki focus her instruction. She scheduled several conferences with Julie. Together they identified the theme in a few picture books and short stories. Julie could do this relatively easily, but didn't have the skills to identify a theme in a longer book. By working with Julie, Franki was able to diagnose the challenge she faced, plan instruction that would support her, and continue to monitor her progress. Franki found that the best approach was to choose very short novels with accessible themes to share with Julie.

Conferences on Characters

Sometimes comments during read-aloud conversations cause us concern. When that happens, we address those concerns in individual conferences. For example, keeping track of characters in books was difficult for Meggie. She was not always sure who was who, and often resorted to asking her classmates for reminders, which bogged down her reading and hindered her comprehension. So, during several conferences, Franki taught her strategies for keeping track of characters independently, such as sketching a picture or writing descriptions of each character as he or she is introduced.

Conferences on Nonfiction

During content area instruction, we recognize students' strengths and challenges in reading nonfiction—more so than at other points during the day. For example, when reading an issue of *Time for Kids*, many of the students were merely skimming the maps and graphs, and didn't seem to be gaining much information from them. During initial whole-class conversations, Franki just listened to students' comments and her fears were confirmed. Many of the students needed help reading maps and graphs. Most had a very narrow understanding of maps, believing that all they do is "tell you where the states are." Another student talked around the pictures on a graph, without recognizing what the information the graph represented or understanding the purpose of graphs. So Franki taught him graph-reading strategies during a few conferences, using the book *Kidbits* (Tesar, Glassman, & Italiano, 1999), which is full of graphs on high-interest topics. Franki and the student looked at each graph, analyzing how it was set up, extracting information from it, and sharing data that was surprising.

When Students Have Something to Teach Us

For students to be part of a reading community outside of school, they need to pay attention to news related to children's books and engage in what we call "literary gossip." They get their information from the *Horn Book*, articles from the local paper about authors, and Web announcements of award-winning books. We share these bits of literary gossip in mini-lessons with students and often follow up with individual conferences.

Franki wasn't aware of *Kira-Kira* (Kadohata, 2004) before it won the Newbery Medal in 2005. She read it quickly over the weekend and brought it to school to share with the class as part of a mini-lesson on the award winners that had recently been announced. She told the class that she thought *Kira-Kira* was okay, but wasn't sure it would have been her choice for the Newbery. She asked if anyone was between books and would like to read it, and Katie rose to the challenge.

Two days later, Katie asked Franki to meet with her about *Kira-Kira*. Franki wasn't sure what to expect, but was ready to help Katie with whatever she needed. It turned out that Katie wanted to teach Franki something! Katie had instantly fallen in love with the book and wanted Franki to understand that it *clearly* should have won the Newbery. She had tabbed several places in the book where the author had used amazing language. She suggested Franki look through her sticky notes to see what she must have missed when she read it. Even though Katie had assessed Franki's needs and met with her to talk about them, Franki also learned a great deal about Katie as a reader. She had never realized just how much Katie paid attention to the ways authors use language in books.

Literary Chitchat

Conferences are not the only times we sit next to a child for a focused conversation. Every conversation that we have with a child, even everyday chitchat, teaches us more about what kind of learner that child is. According to Isabel Beaton, "It's not quite 'accountable' talk, but it's not gossip either. It's not private, but it's also not public. It happens when people are coming together around common work and interests, and transitions are thought about seriously and respectfully" (Beaton, 2000, p. 3).

This kind of literary chitchat happens as students are walking to recess, as they enter the room in the morning, and any time they see that we have a free moment. It is usually initiated by students and inspired by what we have discussed during read-aloud, mini-lessons, small-group work, or traditional conferences. When we pay attention to all of the conversations in a typical day, we are amazed. We consider these conversations to be conferences because we are learning, teaching, and building on what we feel students need as readers.

"Mrs. Sibberson, I finished *Redwall* [Jacques, 1987] last night!" Mei mentioned this to Franki as she was putting away her coat one morning. She was beaming. This book was a fantasy, a new genre for Mei, and therefore a new challenge, and she was feeling good about her accomplishment.

Following a whole-class conversation about the cover illustration of *The Outcasts of 19 Schuyler Place* (Konigsburg, 2004), Christopher approached Franki with an observation he made while previewing a book written by Andrew Clements, one of his favorite authors. Christopher predicted that *Things Not Seen* (2002) was not part of Clements's popular school stories because the cover illustration does not depict a character holding up a large object, as do the covers of the other school storybooks.

Megan came into school one day looking for *Project Mulberry* (Park, 2005) because she had heard about it from a friend on the bus. This was the first time that Megan was excited about a recommendation from a classmate.

Alexandria, who had been having trouble sticking with books, stopped Franki on the way to lunch to tell her that *Snail Mail No More* (Martin & Danziger, 2000) seemed to be a good fit for her. The authors' technique of using letters between the characters to tell the story kept her engaged. She asked if Franki knew of other books like this.

After finishing *The Book Without Words* (Avi, 2005) and discussing the meaning of the green eyes, the class concluded that they symbolized jealousy. Jonathan discovered that Molly Moon in the Molly Moon series also had green eyes and wondered if jealousy was also important in that book. So he mentioned it casually to Franki.

Sterling stopped to ask whether he could use independent reading time to check Amazon.com to determine when the sequel to *Inkheart* (Funke, 2003) would be available.

William asked Franki whether she had a paperback copy of *Children of the Lamp: The Akhenaten Adventure* (Kerr, 2005) because he preferred reading paperbacks over hardcovers.

And Joe ran into the classroom the day after winter break to tell Franki that he had been given a "reading chair" for Christmas.

All of this chitchat gives us new information about our students as readers—and helps us build their profiles.

Conferences Between Students

We often overhear conversations between students as they are lining up for lunch, playing at recess, and getting ready to go home. This is critical to our assessment because the conversations are honest and, therefore, very informative. They tell us what students are doing outside of the routines of the classroom.

For example, when Katie finished reading *Kira-Kira*, she put the book down and said, "That was a sad ending." Brett, who often sat across from Katie as she read, responded, "I knew it would be sad." She looked at him confused.

He replied, "Well, every time you were reading, I could see the whole book. Two girls were on the cover, but at the end of every reading day, you closed the book and the girl on the back part of the cover disappeared and was not with the other girl anymore. So, I knew something bad must happen."

Katie and Franki were stunned by Brett's astute observations. Katie immediately put a sticky note on the cover to remind her to think more about this idea. More important, Franki learned a lot about Brett as a reader. He was paying attention to what classmates were reading *and* using the conversations in read-aloud to help him think about books independently.

Extending Conferences Through Whole-Class Share Time

"It's important for both teachers and kids to remember that group share isn't a show-and-tell session, that it's a purposeful dialogue."

—Nancie Atwell, *In the Middle: Writing, Reading, and Learning With Adolescents* (1987)

We devote the last five to seven minutes of reading workshop to whole-class share time. Years ago, when we started reading workshop, share time was about sharing books. We would recommend books, discuss themes, craft techniques—in general, give kids a place to talk about the books that they were reading. But over time, we realized that this wasn't the most effective way to use this routine because it wasn't teaching students skills and strategies they could use in their own reading.

Now our share time is focused more on students' behaviors as readers. It has become more of a whole-class conference with the child who shares. It has become a time for students to bring their thoughts from independent reading to a whole-class conversation. Students might share things that confuse them, things that delight them, or strategies that are working for them.

This shift is in keeping with our original goal for share time in a reading workshop, which Cora Lee Five and Kathryn Egawa sum up beautifully: "In valuing who our students are, as well as their ideas, we work to establish a sense of community that encourages different points of view and respectful interaction, including students' responses to each other, as well as our responses to students. We demonstrate a respect for their backgrounds and their special ways of learning, and trust that even

> ### Questions We Ask at the Start of Share Time
>
> ◆ Is anyone at a point in their book where they feel totally lost? Tell us about it.
>
> ◆ Is anyone at a point in their book that makes them want to quit?
>
> ◆ Did anyone start a new book today? How do you read differently when you are starting a new book?
>
> ◆ Did anyone try a new type of book today?
>
> ◆ Is anyone figuring out a new way to keep track of characters in their book?

when responses might not seem to make sense, they may indeed be meaningful. It's this kind of environment that allows us to identify and to build upon students' interests and strengths" (1998, p. 1).

In addition to ending reading workshop each day with share time, we occasionally extend invitations to share after mini-lessons, too. For example, a few weeks after her mini-lesson sharing new books with funny characters, Franki asked the class to share their thoughts on any of the books she had recommended. Several days after Brennen's mini-lesson on maintaining the stamina to finish books, Franki asked students if they came up with any other strategies for finishing books.

Questions that we ask at the start of share time are often prompted by the behaviors that we have noticed during our assessments, and our students know that. So they think about and practice new strategies and come to share time prepared to discuss how the strategies are working for them.

Our share time is now more focused. Instead of a free-for-all, it is a true whole-class discussion because we base it on a specific question and invite students to share their thinking about that question. It is a way to extend the conversations that we begin in mini-lessons and read-aloud. Students can hear how classmates are making things work in their own reading.

Furthermore, we use the information that we gather to plan mini-lessons, so share time becomes a great way for us to hear about the students' growth, to anticipate needs that might come up as they try new things, and design whole-class instruction accordingly.

Share time enables us to extend many of the conversations we have with our students. Each share session helps students see new possibilities for future reading. As Leah Mermelstein reminds us in *Don't Forget to Share: The Crucial Last Step in the Writing Workshop* (2007), "Kids not only get to make decisions about what will be taught but also get to choose which parts of the conversation they'll put to use immediately and which parts they'll tuck away for another day. Teachers often ask how to differentiate instruction in the mini-lesson. It's a great question. There are certainly little things we can do in a mini-lesson to address the needs of all our learners, but we can better address their individual needs in a share, where a number of ideas arise naturally, and kids can choose the one that's the best fit for them" (p. 9).

Boards to Extend Thinking From Share Time

In addition to the more traditional share, we found that using boards around the room helps to meet the goals of share time. When an idea comes up in conferences or share time that we feel will benefit the whole class, we create a board for public display. For example, one year Sterling, a fifth grader, noticed several places in his books where italics were used. He became curious about why an author would use italics. During a conference, he asked about this and then shared his question with the class. Knowing that using italics is an important technique, Franki suggested that Sterling start a board in the room labeled "Why Did the Author Use Italics?" to invite others to pay attention to italics during their independent reading time. As his classmates found places where authors had used italics, they added them to the board along with their thinking about why the author had made that choice.

Boards like this serve several purposes. They provide a focused way to extend ideas from share time and other routines. They remind students that our work in those routines can support them in their independent reading. The boards also serve as a reminder for students to pay attention to certain things in their independent reading. Boards have become a way to transform the conversation of mini-lessons and share sessions into something more permanent. Boards help us build on students' strengths.

Possible Topics for Boards

- How did the author use italics and other text features?
- How do authors describe things so you can picture them clearly?
- What do you do when a book you are reading starts out slowly?
- How do you get ready to talk about a book?
- Why did you reread?
- How do you use your reading notebook to build your understanding of a book?

Concluding Thoughts

Whether we meet with students at a table or on the floor, whether the student or the teacher initiates the meeting, whether it is a formal conversation or a quick chat on the way to recess, individual reading conferences are key because they give us individual, focused time with a child. No conference stands alone. They build on one another and on other routines of the reading workshop. Our teaching grows with every assessment we formulate in conferences.

Although we gather information about our students each and every day in the reading workshop, we also assess our students periodically. When we are preparing for parent conferences or determining marks on progress reports, it is helpful to take a wider perspective on assessment. These are times when we want to gather as much evidence as we can, administer more formal assessments, and focus on each student's profile. In the next chapter, we take a look at assessment at key points in the year.

Chapter 8

Reassessing at Key Points in the Year

> "It's very revealing to observe how children grow over time. . . . Their changing abilities, sense of self, and awareness of others remind us to appreciate just how much they are learning and how much their sense of community is increasing."
>
> —Shelley Harwayne, *Going Public: Priorities and Practice at the Manhattan New School* (1999)

There are times during the school year when we want more formal assessments or we want to take a broad look at all the assessments we have accumulated for our students. When we are providing feedback to parents on progress reports or when we are preparing for a student conference, we want to pull together what we have learned about each student's progress as a reader. We want to analyze it more critically than we do on a daily or weekly basis.

It is important to take a close look at each child at these key points during the year. By gathering data, as we did during the first six weeks of school, we document student growth over time and, if necessary, adjust long-term goals for individual students, as well as for the class. We monitor growth over time by looking for patterns in each child's learning. In other words, we compare current assessments to earlier assessments to bring into focus whether our instruction is effective. These assessments often provide evidence of learning we've already observed in our day-to-day work with students, but they also contain surprises. We also take a close look at the progress of the whole class, the effectiveness of our routines and tools, and the way we use time and space in our reading workshop.

Choosing Assessments

We choose the assessments based on two main criteria: whether they'll tell us what we want to know about students and whether they'll help our students understand themselves as readers. When students are aware of their strengths and challenges, they can take responsibility for their growth as readers. Here are some of the assessments we might choose, and their purposes.

Assessment	Purpose
Reading Interview (see pages 54–56)	To determine how students' reading preferences and understanding of the reading process have changed
Developmental Reading Assessment (DRA) (see pages 58–59)	To measure the growth of individual students in accuracy, comprehension, and fluency
	To identify changes and patterns in students who we want to monitor more closely
DRA, Survey Only	To identify changes and patterns in attitudes and beliefs about reading
DRA, Running Record	To measure fluency
Reading Log Reflection (see pages 70–71)	To note book choice, behaviors, and habits
Read-Aloud Notebook (see pages 37–39)	To evaluate use of tools for comprehension
Status of the Class (see pages 53–54)	To monitor reading behaviors
Observations (see pages 28–29)	To note students' participation in routines

We may select a few assessments to administer to the entire class and a few to administer to individual students based on the extent to which we are still monitoring their learning patterns or on our need for information to plan learning experiences that help them meet their challenges. Sometimes these students are still reading below expectations or do not seem engaged during independent reading time. We may also assess students who came to us as strong readers but haven't remained that way. We hope to understand why they are not continuing to grow as readers.

Assessing the Whole Class: Are We Meeting Goals?

In this section, we zero in on six key learning areas: attitudes and behaviors, the definition of reading, choice of genre, written responses, literary essays, and depth of conversations.

Reflecting on Attitudes and Behaviors

One year in January, the students in Franki's class completed a survey before progress report time—the same survey they had completed in September. Franki compared the results of the two surveys for each student, noting growth in their use of strategies and changes in their attitudes and behaviors. She could identify growth in their book choices, their awareness of authors and genres, and their tastes as readers. Students listed specific books, series, and authors, as well as words describing the types of books they enjoyed (e.g., books that are funny or sad, books with some history in them, nonfiction books with photos).

Franki noticed that in September, one student responded that he liked fiction. In January, he was more specific, listing sports fiction as well as authors such as Matt Christopher and Dan Gutman.

Reflecting on the Definition of Reading

It is important to look closely at what's happening in the reading workshop to reflect on how our students define reading.

The Finding

As Franki reviewed the surveys, she noticed that a majority of the students continued to have a limited definition of reading. When students were asked about their strengths and goals, many were still focused on reading out loud and getting the words right. This told Franki that students had a narrow view of what reading was—that it was only about getting the words right.

The Solution

Franki knew that lessons and conversations over the next few weeks had to focus on the larger idea of reading as *thinking* and help students see themselves as readers in much deeper ways. She needed to help each student build an identity as a reader. She chose books that required a great deal of thinking, especially inferring, and contained strong visuals, such as *The Little Red Fish* (Yoo, 2007). She wanted students to experience thinking through a picture book so they could begin to realize that reading was more than getting the words right. Picture books were short enough that they allowed students to experience the process several times in a week.

Reflecting on Choice of Genre

Looking at the kinds of books students are choosing is important if we want them to be well-rounded readers. When students' selections lack variety, it tells us that we have been focused on just one kind of book in mini-lessons or read-aloud. We want our students to read and enjoy a variety of books for a full range of purposes, so we check to see that this is happening at key points in the year.

The Finding

One year, Franki was struck by the fact that very few students listed nonfiction books as a favorite in their DRA surveys. So she collected students' reading logs and looked back at the status-of-the-class notes to see how many students were reading nonfiction. She found that most students were reading *only* fiction during independent reading.

The Solution

Franki began introducing more nonfiction into her students' reading diet by talking honestly with them. She asked them to think hard about themselves as nonfiction readers. From there, for about a week, students reflected on their nonfiction reading, paying attention to the kinds of books they read, magazines they subscribed to, and the topics that they enjoyed reading about. Then they created posters listing their nonfiction reading and a goal they had established. This activity served more than one purpose. First, it helped students (and Franki) see that they actually were nonfiction readers because they all had some type of nonfiction they enjoyed. Second, it provided a great springboard for conversations about nonfiction. With the posters displayed in the classroom, students started talking to one another about books they listed and asking for recommendations from each other.

At around the same time, Franki began a new routine for

Popular Books for Nonfiction Reading Time

- ◆ *The Journey That Saved Curious George* by Louise Borden
- ◆ *Hey Batta Batta Swing! The Wild Old Days of Baseball* by Sally Cook and James Charlton
- ◆ *Albino Animals* by Kelly Milner Hall
- ◆ *Hero Dogs: Courageous Canines in Action* by Donna M. Jackson
- ◆ *Hana's Suitcase* by Karen Levine
- ◆ *Heroes of Baseball: The Men Who Made It America's Favorite Game* by Robert Lipsyte
- ◆ *Balls!* by Michael J. Rosen
- ◆ *What Stinks?* by Marilyn Singer
- ◆ *Transformed: How Everyday Things Are Made* by Bill Slavin
- ◆ *You Wouldn't Want to Explore With Sir Francis Drake! A Pirate You'd Rather Not Know* by Dave Stewart
- ◆ *Girls Think of Everything: Stories of Ingenious Inventions by Women* by Catherine Thimmesh
- ◆ *Gorilla Doctors: Saving Endangered Great Apes* by Pamela S. Turner
- ◆ *The Kid Who Invented the Trampoline: More Surprising Stories About Inventions* by Don Wulffson

nonfiction reading time two mornings each week. She knew that many of her students loved fiction and loved getting lost in a novel. So it would be difficult to ask them to abandon fiction reading for nonfiction reading. Franki took inventory of the nonfiction area of the classroom library and realized that much of the collection was connected to content-area studies. So she found some new books at the library and the bookstore, and then talked up these books, hoping her excitement would be contagious. To increase the chances of getting her kids excited, she devoted the first 15 minutes of the day to independent nonfiction reading. At the end of each week, she invited students to share with classmates any great titles they had found. Within weeks, students were hooked on nonfiction and finding several titles they couldn't wait to read. By allocating a short time each day to nonfiction, students were able to find topics and authors they loved, without giving up fiction. And over time, more nonfiction started to find its way into independent reading time.

Reflecting on Students' Written Responses to Reading

Writing in response to reading is a habit we want all students to develop. We want them to use writing to retell what they read. We want them to be able to share their thinking and opinions in a literary essay. We want them to use writing in ways that help them comprehend their reading (sticky notes, read-aloud notebooks, etc.). And, yes, we want this writing to help them become better test takers.

When we assess students' written responses to reading, we determine a child's understanding of the text, careful to make sure that any problems are directly related to comprehension and not writing skills. For example, when assessing a poor retelling of a story, we may initially think the child doesn't understand the reading. But if we meet with the child, we often find that he can give us a good oral retelling. In that case, we know the child understands the text, and we can work to help him transfer that understanding to his writing.

The Finding

Franki's students were trying out ways to use sticky notes to help them comprehend text based on some strategies that she had modeled. But after a few weeks, Franki noticed that many of her students had abandoned using sticky notes to help them understand the text and were instead using them as bookmarks.

The Solution

Franki thought students might need more guidance using sticky notes in more helpful ways. She decided that different types of sticky notes might help. So she went to the local office-supply store and bought pads of sticky notes in a variety of new colors and shapes. In a mini-lesson, Franki talked with the class about all of the ways that readers think about a text as they read—to ask questions, to write down new, interesting information. She told them frankly that they weren't using sticky notes effectively. Then she showed them all the new sticky notes she had bought, in the shapes of stars, question marks, and more. As she introduced each sticky note, the students talked about how its shape might remind them of what strategy they could use. The question mark, for example, could be used to flag questions the reader wants to hold on to. From there, he could mark the page number where the question was answered in the story. The star could be used to flag things the reader thinks might relate to the book's theme, such as phrases that come up over and over again. The shapes of the sticky notes encouraged students to pay closer attention to the ways they were thinking about text. By matching the shape of the sticky note to their thinking, students were able to use their writing to think in new ways about text. In time, they did not need the variety of sticky notes to apply strategies. They did it on their own, automatically.

Franki witnessed Haylie using sticky notes in a different, but equally effective way. Haylie was reading a few books from the A–Z Mysteries series, using the map in the front of each book to help her track clues to the mystery. She and Franki worked together to mark with sticky notes places in the text where map locations were mentioned so that Haylie could go back to those places as needed. Franki asked Haylie to share this strategy with the class the next day, and many students found it useful.

Reflecting on Literary Essays

After completing a book in read-aloud, Franki sometimes asks her students to pay attention to the ideas and questions that linger in their minds. Sometimes she asks students to write an essay on one of those ideas or questions. Early in the year, students tend to write about plot, but as the year progresses, they write about bigger issues.

The Finding

While reviewing essays one year, Franki realized that students had strong opinions and had done a good job of supporting those opinions with information from the text. William wrote that he believed the title *Because of Winn-Dixie* did not fit the book. He believed that Opal, the main character, did not make friends because of her new pet, Winn-Dixie. Instead, he argued that Opal had done this on her own because she was a strong person, citing some examples to support his point. Although William was headed in the right direction, Franki felt he could use some direct quotes for further support.

The Solution

Franki introduced ways for students to collect quotes, using picture books. Then she asked students to go back to the read-aloud book they were writing about and find passages that helped support their thinking. She gave them lots of time to practice this skill.

Reflecting on Depth of Conversations

We always listen closely to classroom conversations, but we listen especially closely when we are preparing for progress reports or parent conferences. We might discover that students who did not participate earlier in the year are now actively participating. We might notice jumps in the level of sophistication in a child's conversation. We listen for ways conversations have changed over time.

The Finding

One year during read-aloud, Franki was disappointed by the level of students' conversations. The discussions lacked depth and evidence of a clear understanding of the reading. So she decided to listen closely for three days and take notes on the kinds of comments students were making. She found that they were tracking character changes, thinking about the book's theme, and asking good questions, but they weren't going deeper. Franki was most concerned about the fact that the students were not supporting their thinking with evidence from the text.

The Solution

When Franki looked back at her notes from earlier in the year, she realized that just 12 weeks before, most students had been only making predictions during read-aloud. She had almost forgotten how far they had come in such a short time. She had chosen books to help them move beyond predictions, and the students had met that goal. As teachers, we are often so busy looking ahead, that we don't take the time to look back and celebrate the strides our students make. Periodic assessments enable us to celebrate *and* set new goals. By looking back on her notes for a specific purpose, Franki could move students toward deeper thinking while acknowledging the impressive growth they had made.

Assessing Individual Students: Are They Making Progress?

While it's important to assess the growth of the whole class at key points in the year, it's also important to assess the growth of individual children using the Developmental Reading Assessment (DRA), which gives us a standardized way to measure growth. We can look at fluency, comprehension, and other important areas of reading over a wide range. But we have to look at more than the final numbers on the test. We must also look closely at accuracy, fluency, and comprehension, comparing these results to results from earlier in the year to see exactly where and how the child is progressing and how to set goals and plan instruction.

Assessing Routines: Are They Working?

Once we have assessed students and their progress, we reconsider the reading workshop routines we have established—read-aloud, independent reading, conferring, mini-lessons, and small-group instruction—and think about how they are meeting the needs of students.

Independent Reading

◆ What types of books are students choosing?

◆ Do most students have favorite authors?

◆ Which students are still not engaged during independent reading time?

◆ Which students continually get lost between books, and are unsure about what to read next?

◆ Who is stuck in a series, author, or genre? Does it help or limit the child?

◆ How is the quality of discussion about reading among the children?

◆ Are students using the various boards in the classroom? How?

Read-Aloud

◆ Is the level of conversation during read-aloud higher than it was?

◆ How has it changed?

◆ How are students using their reading notebooks?

◆ Do notebooks and conversations help students with comprehension?

Small-Group Instruction

◆ Which groups have been most effective? Why?

◆ Which groups have not been effective? Why not?

◆ Are most students signing up for groups that meet their needs?

Individual Reading Conferences

◆ Are students initiating reading conferences?

◆ What topics are addressed in conferences?

◆ What are students noticing about their own reading?

We think about the patterns that surface and consider future instruction. How can we build on what is going well to help students deal with challenges that remain? How can we use the routines we have established to move individual students forward?

Routines to Support Individual Students

It's also important to look at the way routines are working for individual students. Is each routine helping the child become a better reader? Can we provide better support during some or all of the routines?

For example, Julia, an English-language learner, is one of the students we monitor more closely at key points in the year. Julia has made good progress since school began, and there are now a few areas that she can work on to move forward.

◆ Julia now has favorite books and authors. She enjoys the Bailey School Kids series. We know that series books are good for her at this stage in her development because the characters and setting are usually the same in all books. Because she is comfortable with characters and setting, she can focus more on understanding the plot.

- As we look at her DRA and state assessment for comprehension, we find that retelling is difficult for Julia. She can retell a story, but in a disorganized way. We are not sure whether this is because of Julia's limited English skills or because she does not have a good sense of story elements. So we continue to monitor her progress.
- Julia is always very engaged during read-aloud, but keeping track of the story is difficult for her. Julia uses her read-aloud notebook to summarize and make predictions. But because of her difficulties with following plot, using her notebook to keep track of characters might help.
- In her independent reading, Julia reads simple books like *Judy Moody* in their entirety but often abandons books that are more difficult. When reading books that are right for her, she often laughs aloud and shares passages with others. She enjoys reading when she understands what is happening in the story.
- She reads a great deal in her native language, and as we've seen in read-aloud, she knows when things aren't making sense.

After thinking long and hard about all of this information, we decide to focus on Julia's comprehension by working with her on retelling stories orally, gaining vocabulary, and learning the parts of a story. By working on oral retellings, we can help her transfer what she has learned to written retellings. Here is how we will support her in each routine:

Read-Aloud

We will continue to encourage Julia to tell us what is confusing her. We will invite her into the conversation more often when we are focusing on plot and characters. We will also make a point of calling on Julia to remind us of what happened in the story yesterday, before we start the day's reading.

Independent Reading

When we meet with Julia during conferences, we might share comprehension strategies with her, such as summarizing each day's reading on a sticky note and reading that note before she begins the next day's reading.

Small-Group Instruction

We want Julia to begin talking with others about books she is reading independently, because it will help her think through the plot and characters. We will place Julia in groups that are discussing popular books, learning about story elements, focusing on vocabulary, and sharing good books for independent reading.

Assessing the Tools in Reading Workshop: Do They Support Comprehension?

We provide read-aloud notebooks, sticky notes, and two-column charts to our students so they have options for understanding complex books. Our goal isn't that they necessarily use the tools on the spot. Rather, we want them to be able to use the tools when they need them.

Read-Aloud Notebooks

Read-aloud notebooks, for example, show students how writing can help them understand a text at a deeper level. When we look at reading notebook samples, we do not focus on the product, but rather on the *process*. Do students have a better understanding of the text *because* of their use of the tool? Taking time to see how the entire class is using read-aloud notebooks is critical to assessing the range of responses and the overall depth of thinking.

When assessing read-aloud notebooks and other written pieces, we don't want to encourage jumping through hoops and playing the game of school, as described in Chapter 1. If we truly want students to use read-aloud notebooks to track and refine their thinking, we must give them the message that the notebook is for them. The minute we mandate what we expect to see in the notebook, the child loses ownership of it. So we need to be careful to assess notebooks in ways that inform our teaching. We must determine how the strategies in the notebook support reading comprehension.

One year, Franki gave students small, spiral read-aloud notebooks to be used exclusively during the reading of *Crash* (Spinelli, 1996). After the reading, she collected the notebooks to determine whether students were using the notebook to understand the text more deeply. Because the *Crash* notebook was separate, Franki could easily collect and compare them and look for patterns in the way students used the notebooks. She could also keep notebook pages as a midyear sample from each student.

The Finding

As Franki reviewed the notebooks, she noticed that students continued to be most comfortable with the strategy of making predictions. But she also noticed that several students were attempting to collect information in charts. Although the idea was a good one, the charts were not necessarily supporting their reading. Franki wanted to help students to create charts that more effectively supported their understanding. When students first learn a strategy, they usually use it in simple ways until they get more support.

The Solution

Franki planned a few mini-lessons on strategies for recording data on charts. Since some students were tracking changes in a character, Franki worked with them to help them determine the kinds of evidence that shows changes in a character. Other students had written predictions without stating reasons for them. Franki showed those students how to set up the charts so that they could include more text-specific information. Students went back to old charts they had created and thought of ways that they could have made them more useful. In quick conferences at the beginning of subsequent read-alouds, Franki pushed students to add to their charts.

read the book before.

I read the book!

3/14

The miraculas jurney of Edward Tulane

Keeping track of mood

always sad when he goes away

Mood	Sentance/words	Chapter #
Bored	Staring straight into Egypt st.	#1
Mad	"What's this bunny dong here!"	#2
		#3
		#4
		#6
Sad	I am now so far away from the stars.	#7
appreciated	Put him sitting in a place he liked	#7
Happy	So happy not reffered to "it"	#7
Horrified	He did not want to be a girl.	#9
Happy	a dress wont bother me	#9
mad	A Hatred for Lolly	#10
Happy	Edward was happy	#10
sad	felt like crying	#14
Loved	I have been loved he told the stars	#15
Mad / Scared	The Pelligrina Crow	#15
Very Sad	I want Sarah Ruth. My heart is broken	#19
Mad	Play with me all you want	#21
No Mood	Edwards world went black	#21

Students designed charts to help them collect information during read-aloud. These charts were helpful in analyzing various issues in the books.

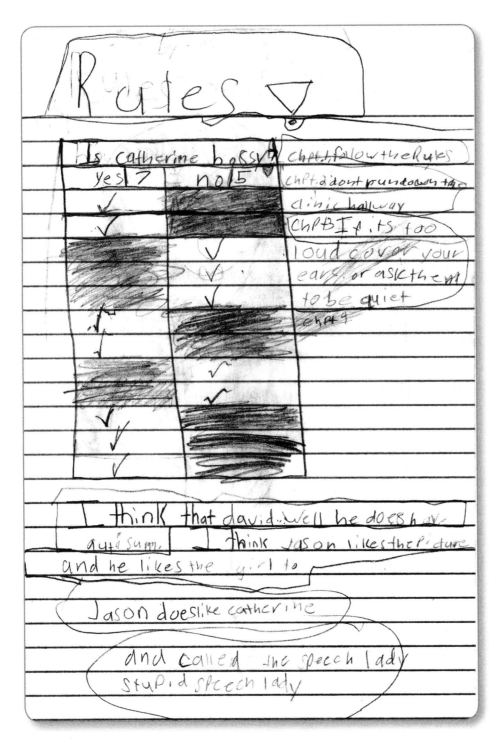

Rules ▽

Is catherine bossy?		chpt. follow the Rules
yes 7	no 5	chpt. dont run down the clinic hallway
✓		chpt B If its too loud cover your ears or ask them to be quiet
✓	✓	chp 4
	✓	
	✓	
✓		
✓	✓	
✓		
✓		

I think that david. well he does have autism.   I think Jason likes the picture
and he likes the girl to

Jason does like catherine

and called the speech lady
stupid speech lady

The Finding

Another year, while reviewing student notebooks, Franki discovered that some students were not using a variety of strategies. While she saw a few good uses of the notebook as a tool for understanding, such as sketching characters, she noticed that most students were not using notebooks in a variety of ways, despite the variety of books they were being exposed to. In other words, as a class, students were using a range of strategies, but individually, they were not.

The student's notebook entry reads:

The Miraculous Journey of Edward Tulane

Place and ... what I Think	
His House	I Think That he is going to get up and get something to eat
a ship	I Think Edward is going to fall into the ocean
Ocean	I Think The fisherman is going to cash him
Bottom of The ocean	I Think he's going to change each place he goes on his Journey
green ship heley	I Think heley is related to ... so heley gives it to ...
Thash	I Think he will go to The Junck yard and the junck yard Person will Take him home

The Solution

Franki asked students to look through their notebooks and find an entry that really helped them to understand the text. From there, the class created a display of their chosen notebook entries, and students shared strategies with one another. When the wall space was needed for something else, Franki compiled the entries into a book that students could refer to when their notebook work became stale and ineffective. Franki used the thinking of individual students to help *all* students.

Reporting Growth

It is important for teachers to have an opportunity to report growth to students and parents. We are always providing daily feedback to students and keeping parents informed about their child's progress. We schedule parent conferences so we can review a child's progress and the evidence we have for growth. We don't want our students to think that parent conferences are secret meetings and have them wonder about what we might say about them as learners. If we are serious about having our students be an important part of the assessment process, they must participate in the reflection process. Although self-reflection is part of our daily and weekly work with students, we believe that students also need to look at their growth over long-term intervals. When students do this, they are often surprised by their growth.

We want students equally involved in preparing for progress reports so they can understand their purpose and how they can help in setting goals for future learning. We include students in the process in the hope that they see the progress report as a summary of their work during the trimester and, ultimately, a key to their growth as readers.

Progress Reports: Time for Student Self-Assessment

In our district, progress reports are sent home every 12 weeks, three times a year. As the end of a trimester nears, we ask students to spread out their reading logs, reading notebooks, previews from read-aloud, their contributions to the displays around the room, written responses, and other evidence of learning and look for positive and negative patterns and evidence of growth, for 30 to 40 minutes, with friends and on their own. We gather students together to share what they've learned about themselves. This helps them sharpen their thinking and benefit from each other's thinking. Here are some observations students might make:

- I used to only read the Magic Treehouse. Now I read other series too.
- I like to follow changes in characters in books during read-aloud.
- Earlier in the year, I had trouble figuring out the theme of our read-aloud books. Now, it is easier for me.
- I seem to get stuck on an author for a long time.
- I don't read much poetry.
- It is easier for me to write about books we've read in read-aloud.
- I focus mostly on characters in my read-aloud notebook.
- I have new strategies for understanding articles in *Time for Kids.*
- I've tried sticky notes to help me record important information.

We build on these conversations to form groups, set goals, and share growth with parents. But these conversations are also valuable in that they set the stage for progress reports. From there, we gather even more information for progress reports in end-of-trimester conferences with students.

End-of-Trimester Conferences With Students

We often talk with each of our students about her progress and goals for the coming months in an end-of-the-trimester conference. We do this for several reasons. First, it gives us an extended period of time—up to a half hour—to understand how the student sees herself as a reader. Second, it allows the student to weigh in on the subject of grades and progress reports. Finally, it gives the student the language to talk honestly with her parents about her progress report when it is sent home.

We give students a day or two to prepare for the conference by gathering evidence of their reading growth, such as use of strategies, variety of texts read, and more sophisticated written responses. Some students don't recognize their own growth as clearly as we do. Others recognize it so well they are able to shed light on things we have missed. After we've talked in depth, matching our evidence to the student's, the student understands his progress and can more easily articulate it to his parents when reports go home. If time allows, our students write a letter to go along with their progress report, outlining their reflections about their growth and goals for the trimester. Parents often respond with their own observations, questions, and goals.

Because we devote 30 minutes to each student, it is often difficult to schedule conferences. Some years, we extend independent reading time to 60 minutes from the usual 30 to 45 minutes for two to three weeks, and meet with two students a day. Other years, we've had an All Day Read, where students come in with sleeping bags, pillows, magazines, and books, and dig in while we conduct conferences. An All Day Read allows us to get through most of the class's conferences.

We begin to notice patterns in strengths and challenges after talking long and hard with each child for a concentrated period of time. The notes we take from these long conferences are often useful in quick conferences later in the year to help students clarify goals and address needs.

Grading

As required by our district, we give students letter grades in grades 4 and 5 for each content area. We also give marks for each of the state standards to let students and parents know whether they are meeting them. For each standard, students receive an AC if they are achieving expectations for that standard, a PR if they are progressing toward achieving the standard, and an LP if there is limited progress.

We measure growth *toward* the standards instead of in isolation. For example, one of our state standards is for the student to understand a variety of genres. We look for evidence that shows that each student is gaining skills in that area. Another goal is for the student to choose appropriate books, so we look for evidence of growth in that area.

To figure out grades, we have to look at students' work over time. Because we do so many day-to-day assessments, we have an abundance of evidence to help us. Our daily routines provide many examples of students' work from the following sources:

- Read-aloud notebook
- Reading log
- Written responses to reading
- Notes from big question talks
- Notes from conferences
- Status-of-the-class forms
- Reflection sheets
- Student sticky notes
- Notes from mini-lessons

We use a sheet for summarizing how well each student performs in each classroom routine. Under each routine, we list accomplishments that the student has completed during the trimester, as well as what is working for the student. We then assign a point scale for each routine, and then calculate the points into a percent and a grade. This sheet often becomes the basis for the end-of-the-trimester conference. We confer with each student and look at evidence of growth in reading, using the sheet to keep the discussion on track.

For years, what we valued was not what we graded. We would grade a student's understanding of the book, rather than how well the student applied a strategy. Grading a student's application of a skill or strategy is difficult because it is not as easy to measure. But we must do it in order for teaching and assessment to be productive and authentic.

For example, if students do not write in their notebooks during read-aloud time, Franki might consider giving them a low number in that area. She changed her thinking on this one year when she met with Kelly, who told her that she could only write new thinking after she had talked to a friend. During the end-of-trimester conference, Franki realized that Kelly was very engaged in the conversation and that, sometimes, writing actually interfered with her comprehension. Although Kelly wasn't using her read-aloud notebook effectively, she was using conversation as a tool to support her comprehension. So the measure of progress could no longer be based on the read-aloud notebook alone. Franki worked on helping Kelly use her read-aloud notebook in a way that was comfortable for her, but she gave Kelly all of the points for read-aloud because she was meeting the goal of trying new ways of thinking to support her understanding.

It is often hard to stay focused on these bigger goals when assigning grades. Was Franki assessing how Kelly gained strategies in comprehension or how she jumped through the hoops to fill in her read-aloud notebook "correctly"? Without the conversation with Kelly, Franki would have done the latter.

As part of the grading process, we ask students to fill out reflection sheets on their learning, with evidence to support what they write. When students provide this evidence and explain their growth, it is easy to see how they are meeting goals.

We are careful to look at more than one example of a strategy or skill when assigning

Second Trimester Reading Grade   Total Points _____/**335**
                                                      ____ % Grade:_____

_____Read Daily   50 pts.
    Do you have your book?
    Do you choose good books that you stick with?
    Do you read a variety of genres?
    Are you engaged during Reading Workshop?

_____ Reading Logs   10 pts.
    Home Reading Log
    School Reading Log

_____Know self as reader/self reflection   10 pts.

_____Literary thinking in Independent Reading   50 pts.

_____Read Aloud Discussion   25 pts.
    Do you participate in discussions?
    Do you keep notes that help you understand the book better?
    Do you try new things in your reader's notebook?
    Do you change/grow your thinking based on what
        others say in the discussion?

_____Essays/Big Questions/Write in response to reading   40 pts.
    Do your essays reflect your understanding of your reading?
    Do you focus on a deeper understanding of the text?

_____Reading Minilessons   40 pts.
    Do you use comprehension strategies to help you understand
    text?

_____Time For Kids   20 pts.
    Are you using features of nonfiction text to help you understand?

_____Comprehension Minilessons   40 points
    Did you try the strategies to help you understand?
    Were you successful in using the strategies?

_____Book Clubs   50 points
    Have you joined 1—2 book clubs?
    Do you prepare in a way that supports understanding?
    Does the talk help you think more deeply about the book?

An example of one trimester's score sheet for grading purposes.

grades. Because Kelly was more comfortable talking about her thinking during read-aloud than writing about it *and* she had the opportunity to bring that to Franki's attention, Franki paid closer attention to the kinds of discussions Kelly was having about texts during small-

Name **Alex S**

Reading Reflection—First Trimester Reflection

List the books that you finished this trimester (home and school).
Artemis Fowl 1, Duble Fudge, On The far
Side of The Mountain, Artemis 2, Artemis Fowl 3,
Dragon Slayer 1,2,3,4,5, 6, 7, 8, 9, 10. and Riseing
Stars

List any books that you read part of—or that you quit before you were finished.
Artemis Fowl 4, Frindle and The Report Card

Did you find any new authors/series that you like?
Kate McMullan, Geronimo Stilton, Jean Craighead
and Eoin Colfer

List all of the different genres that you've read. Do you think that you read a good variety?
Fiction, Fantasy and Non Fiction

It is important to think ahead in your reading. List the books that you plan to read sometime soon. How did you hear about them?
The rest of Dragon Slayers Academy and
Start Spider Wick. Brett and Willoam
told me about the books, when I was
looking for books to read

What are you most proud of in your reading this trimester?
I've been reading alot more books
then I did last and in the
Summer.

What is a goal that you have for your reading next trimester?
• To try to read more.
• Read harder books.
• Read longer books.

This reflection sheet helps students think about their growth during read-aloud.

group and whole-class instruction. By combining all of this knowledge, Franki could effectively assess the skills and strategies and help Kelly improve on them as necessary.

At the end of the trimester, we think about how much each child has grown and we set new goals for each child. We have been collecting evidence of growth throughout the

Day-to-Day Assessment in the Reading Workshop

Choose a book that you read this trimester (December/January/February). Think about and answer the following questions. This could be a book that you read independently or one that you read for a book talk with classmates.

Title of Book Things Not Seen

Author Andrew Clements

Genre Fiction

Which character in the book was the protagonist? How do you know? How did the character change over the course of the book? Use specific examples to support your thinking.

The protagonist in the book is boby, because he is the person who is always there ? Also he is the one who has the problem. (He has a fowe probles on the side too)

The characator changed by his proble, whitch is him trends invisabile. He chang'd by meting a girl that he wond not normble pay ateson to. The girl was bloid ? he was invisable, so she did not care that he was invrsable.

So I think he lernd the lesen that you do not need to see a friend to no a friend.

What was the setting of the book? What did the setting have to do with the story? Why do you think the author chose this particular setting?

The setting was his home. I think the ather chose this setting because home is were alot of things happen ? It was a wome ? relasing setiny because the story needed one comforbic ? relasing pale so the story wond not be to follof actson

What was the problem in the story? List the things that happened (in order) to solve the problem?

The proble was he treade inviable.

To soule the problem there were some tecknifie things frist bobys friend e-malcs boby ? his friend told him to sleep with this eletic blackt ? then at 4:30 a latey comes because boby has been out of school for a log time so boby take all his clows of ? <the latey comes up <? he is visable>

This form invites students to reflect on the literary terms they learned during the trimester.

trimester. As we pull these artifacts together and invite students to share their own evidence, we determine how much each of them has progressed. We analyze their learning over time as we think about future goals. We find that this method of grading provide more evidence than we have ever had before.

Read Aloud

How did read aloud help you as a reader? Explain.

It helps me understand more, about the book then me trying to read it by my self.

Rate the books—put them in order and share what you learned from each one.
(Use a separate sheet of paper to cut and paste them in order.)

Which book had the biggest impact on you and/or your reading? Why?

The bad begining because sottove easy and I really like his books

Responses
Read through this section. What do you notice? What did you learn as a reader?

That long books aren't always harder tham short books.

What are you most proud of in your reading this year?

That I don't waset time act by like sitting and i'm reading

What goals do you have for your reading?

To read 30 pages or more.

Alex S,

Reading Notebook

Me as a Reader

Read through your first entries. How have you changed as a reader?

I've been picking better spots, I haven't been sitting by my friends and i've been reading more.

Reading Log

Look through your reading log. What do you notice about your reading over the year?

at the beginning of the year I wasn't reading alot but now I am reading alot more than I used to.

How have you changed?

I used to sit by my friends and talk but now I sit away from my friends and I read.

What are you most proud of?

that i've been finishing books faster and reading alot more pages.

Which books did you read that changed you or helped you as a reader? How?

Mouse and the Motorcycle because it's funny and I hooked on to it after the first couple of chapters.

These forms help students reflect on several areas of reading.

Concluding Thoughts

The end of each trimester is a good time for teachers to reflect. As we gather evidence of student growth to complete progress reports, we can ask ourselves questions like these: What is working for each student? Which routines seem to be confusing to students? What should I change? Are there any patterns emerging across several students' work? Just as we did after the first six weeks, we look hard at individual students and the class as a whole. But we also take the opportunity to look at our teaching, the resources we are using, the learning that is happening, and the gaps that reveal themselves.

Our most important role is helping students move toward independence. To accomplish that, we need to reflect to make sure we are doing everything we can to support the young readers in our classroom. We strive to give every one of them opportunities to grow and learn.

Conclusion

> " The challenge in writing about assessment is that assessment happens in so many ways, for so many purposes, that is hard to pin down. Assessment is the thinking teacher's mind work. It is the intelligence that guides our every moment as a teacher. "
>
> —Lucy Calkins, *A Guide to the Writing Workshop (2006)*

The two of us have spent most of our professional lives alongside readers in grades 3 to 6. We have watched children learn and grow into independent learners. It has been a lifelong celebration of learning.

Karen is the principal of a new school finishing its first year. Children, parents, and teachers began the year with so many hopes and dreams and now it's a time for them to share memories and reflect. The oldest students' time in elementary school is coming to a close, and in a few months they will enter middle school. This is both an ending and a new beginning.

We think about what Carol Jago tells us: "Books have been my surest source of pleasure and interest my whole life long. Doesn't it follow that I should want the same for my students? Of course. But the challenge is to make sure my classroom practice doesn't send them the opposite message" (2005, p. 54).

We hope this book helps readers think about classroom practices and the big messages we send our students. We hope our readers consider the importance of a reading workshop and the predictable routines that help students move toward independence. We hope our readers recognize that teaching and day-to-day assessments can be the foundation for the most authentic learning for our students.

We know that moving children toward independence can be as simple as planting the seed of an idea in a conversation and waiting for the students to take hold of the idea and make it a part of the shared wisdom of the classroom. But it is the thoughtful teacher who knows what seeds to plant. As the teacher creates profiles of students, their reading strengths and challenges become clear. Teachers encourage a learning climate that supports the diversity of learners and learning styles in the classroom. They plan the most thoughtful and authentic learning experiences because they pay attention to the day-to-day assessments that they make. The cycle of learning and growing together is never-ending.

Status of the Class

Name_____

Date	Title	Page

Day-to-Day Assessment in the Reading Workshop © 2008 Franki Sibberson and Karen Szymusiak, Scholastic. An explanation of how to use this reproducible appears on pages 53–54.

Reading Interview

Name_____   Date_____

How would you describe yourself as a reader?

What are you currently reading?

What kinds of things did you read over the summer?

What kinds of things do you like to read?

What kinds of things do you NOT like to read?

Do you read any magazines or newspapers?

Is there a series that you like to read? Why?

Do you have a favorite author?

Do you have a favorite book?

What are you going to read next?

Day-to-Day Assessment in the Reading Workshop © 2008 Franki Sibberson and Karen Szymusiak, Scholastic. An explanation of how to use this reproducible appears on pages 54–56.

How do you choose the books you read?

Do you talk to anyone about the books you read? Who?

What do the other people in your family read?

What kinds of books do your friends read?

What do you do when you get stuck?

What do you do when you start to read each day?

How do you keep track of the characters in the books you are reading?

What kind of reading is easy for you?

What kind of reading is hard for you?

What are you most proud of in your reading?

Day-to-Day Assessment in the Reading Workshop © 2008 Franki Sibberson and Karen Szymusiak, Scholastic. An explanation of how to use this reproducible appears on pages 54–56.

Assessment Web

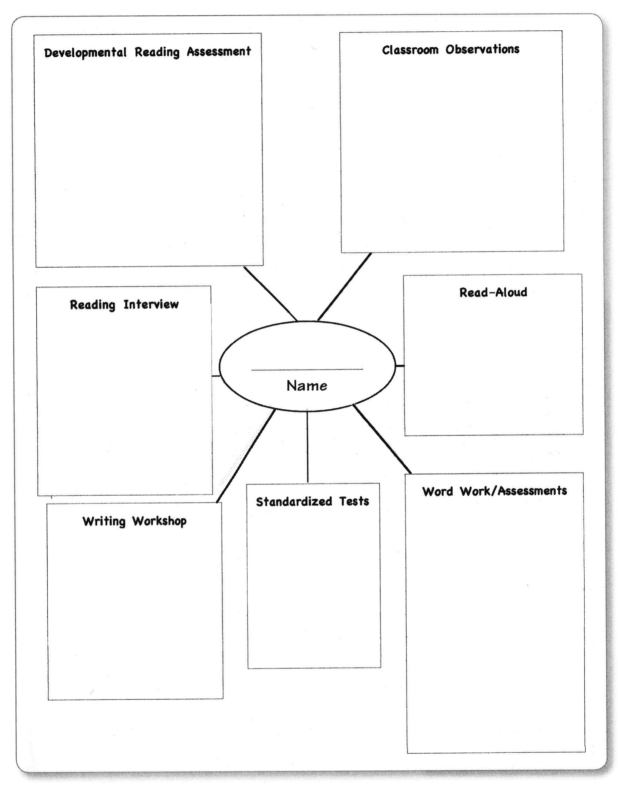

School Reading Log

Name_____

Date	Title	Page

Day-to-Day Assessment in the Reading Workshop © 2008 Franki Sibberson and Karen Szymusiak, Scholastic. An explanation of how to use this reproducible appears on page 68–69.

Reading Log Reflection Sheet

Name_____   Date_____

Use your reading log to answer the following questions:

When looking at your log, what do you notice about your reading?

Are you reading a variety of books or are you stuck in a genre?

Do you have some idea of the books you want to read after you finish your current book? Which books might you read?

How do you choose books? What are some ways that you decide which books to read next?

Which books have you quit? Was that a good decision? Why or why not?

Do you have anything you want to work on in the way you choose books?

Day-to-Day Assessment in the Reading Workshop © 2008 Franki Sibberson and Karen Szymusiak, Scholastic. An explanation of how to use this reproducible appears on page 70.

Home Reading Reflection Sheet

Name_____   Date_____

Look over your home and school reading logs so far this year.
What do you notice about your school reading? List 3–5 things.

What do you notice about your home reading? List 3–5 things.

How have you changed as a reader so far this year?

What are you most proud of in your reading?

What would you like to improve on in your reading?

Day-to-Day Assessment in the Reading Workshop © 2008 Franki Sibberson and Karen Szymusiak, Scholastic. An explanation of how to use this reproducible appears on pages 74–75.

Summer Reading Plan

Name_____   Date_____

Which books have you heard about that you may want to read?

Which authors have you enjoyed this year?

Which genre are you enjoying right now?

Is there a book or a kind of book that you didn't have time to read this year that you'd like to read this summer?

Do you have a goal for summer reading?

When and where might you read over the summer?

Day-to-Day Assessment in the Reading Workshop © 2008 Franki Sibberson and Karen Szymusiak, Scholastic. An explanation of how to use this reproducible appears on page 76.

Read-Aloud Notebook Reflection Sheet #1

Name_____   Date_____

Choose one page or entry from your reading notebook. Find one that you are especially proud of because your writing and thinking helped you to understand something better. Explain below why you chose this entry. Be specific.

Day-to-Day Assessment in the Reading Workshop © 2008 Franki Sibberson and Karen Szymusiak, Scholastic. An explanation of how to use this reproducible appears on pages 90–92.

Read-Aloud Notebook Reflection Sheet #2

Name_____   Date_____

During our read-aloud of _____ by _____,
you wrote or sketched in your notebook to help you understand the text. What kinds of writing/
sketching did you do during the reading and discussion of the book?

How did writing/sketching help your thinking and understanding of the book?

What new strategy might you try in your notebook for one of our next read-alouds? Did you see
anyone do anything that might work for you?

Group Goal Reflection Sheet

Name_____   Date_____

Which reading workshop group or groups did you sign up for?

Why did you decide to sign up for each group?

How do you hope these groups will help you as a reader?

Do you have any other reading goals?

Day-to-Day Assessment in the Reading Workshop © 2008 Franki Sibberson and Karen Szymusiak, Scholastic. An explanation of how to use this reproducible appears on pages 126–127.

Thinking Ahead in Reading

Name_____   Date_____

What are three things that will help you the most as a reader?

Which skills and strategies do you need to become an even better reader?

Which of the skills do you think is the most important for you right now? Why do you think so?
Be specific.

How might a group help you with each of your goals? What are you hoping to gain from a group
focusing on these skills and strategies?

Day-to-Day Assessment in the Reading Workshop © 2008 Franki Sibberson and Karen Szymusiak, Scholastic. An
explanation of how to use this reproducible appears on pages 126–127.

Sticking With a Book

Name_____   Date_____

Book Title	Date	Easy or Hard?	Why?

Day-to-Day Assessment in the Reading Workshop © 2008 Franki Sibberson and Karen Szymusiak, Scholastic. An explanation of how to use this reproducible appears on page 131.

Plan for Reading Discussion Group

Name_____   Date_____

What book or piece of writing will you be reading and discussing with your group?

How did you decide on this book?

Why does this book or piece interest you?

Why do you think the book is worth talking about?

List the members of your group.

When will your group meet?

How will you prepare for the discussion?

Day-to-Day Assessment in the Reading Workshop © 2008 Franki Sibberson and Karen Szymusiak, Scholastic. An explanation of how to use this reproducible appears on page 139–140.

Discussion Group Reflection Sheet

Name_____   Date_____

As you get ready to meet with your group, what are some issues you'd like to discuss? Which things can your group help you to understand better? (You can use sticky notes and other tools to mark these places to help get the conversation started.)

When you met with your group for the first time, what are some things that you decided to discuss as a group?

As you talked, how did your thinking about an issue change or grow? Be specific.

What was the most significant part of the discussion for you?

How did participating in a group help you as a reader?

Day-to-Day Assessment in the Reading Workshop © 2008 Franki Sibberson and Karen Szymusiak, Scholastic. An explanation of how to use this reproducible appears on pages 139–140.

Book Club Reflection Sheet

Name_____   Date_____

Before the Discussion

How did you prepare for your book club?

What are some things you'd like to discuss?

After the Discussion

What was the most important thing that was discussed? Why was it interesting or important?

Did someone in the group say something that changed or added to your original thinking about the book? Describe it.

Did someone share an idea that was new to you—something you had not thought about on your own? Explain.

How did participating in this book talk add to what you know about books and reading?

Day-to-Day Assessment in the Reading Workshop © 2008 Franki Sibberson and Karen Szymusiak, Scholastic. An explanation of how to use this reproducible appears on pages 139–140.

Trimester Reading Grade

Total Points _____/325

_____% Grade:_____

Name_____   Date_____

_____Read Daily   50 points
    Do you have your book?
    Do you choose good books that you stick with?
    Do you read a variety of genres?
    Are you engaged during independent reading?

_____Reading Logs   10 points
    Home reading log
    School reading log

_____ Literary Thinking Reflection   50 points
    Did you understand all elements of the plot?

_____Read-Aloud Discussion   25 points
    Do you participate in discussions?
    Do you keep notes that help you understand the book better?
    Do you try new strategies?
    Do you change your thinking based on what others say in the discussion?

_____Essay/Big Questions Writing   50 points
    Do your essays reflect your understanding of the reading?
    Do you focus on getting a deeper understanding of the text?
    Is your writing clear and organized?

_____Reading Mini-Lessons   50 points
    Did you participate in mini-lessons?
    Do you show evidence of practicing skills taught in mini-lessons?
    Have you found strategies that work for you?

_____ *Time for Kids*   40 points
    Are you using features of nonfiction text to support your comprehension?

_____Book Clubs   50 points
    Have you joined at least one book club?
    Do you prepare to discuss the book?
    Do these talks help you understand the book?

Reading Log—Trimester Reflection

Name_____   Date_____

List the books that you finished this trimester (at home and school).

List any books that you read but quit before you finished.

Did you find any new authors or series that you like?

List all the different genres you read.

Is there a book that you'd like to read next trimester?

What are you most proud of in your reading?

Do you have a goal for next trimester?

Day-to-Day Assessment in the Reading Workshop © 2008 Franki Sibberson and Karen Szymusiak, Scholastic. An explanation of how to use this reproducible appears on pages 175–177.

Thinking About Literary Elements

Name_____   Date_____

Choose a book that you read this trimester. Think about and answer the following questions. This could be a book that you read independently or one that you read for a book talk with classmates.

Title of Book_____
Author_____
Genre_____

Which character in the book was the protagonist? How do you know? How did the character change over the course of the book? Use specific examples to support your thinking.

What was the setting of the book? What did the setting have to do with the story? Why do you think the author chose this particular setting?

What was the problem in the story? List the things that happened (in order) to solve the problem.

Who tells the story—one of the characters or a narrator? List reasons you think the author made the decision.

What is one of the main themes in the book? Why do you think so?

Day-to-Day Assessment in the Reading Workshop © 2008 Franki Sibberson and Karen Szymusiak, Scholastic. An explanation of how to use this reproducible appears on pages 175–177.

Professional Resources Cited

Angelillo, J. (2003). *Writing about reading: From book talk to literary essays, grades 3–8.* Portsmouth, NH: Heinemann.

Atwell, N. (1987). *In the middle: Writing, reading, and learning with adolescents.* Portsmouth, NH: Boynton/Cook.

Atwell, N. (2007). *The reading zone: How to help kids become skilled, passionate, habitual, critical readers.* New York: Scholastic.

Beaton, I. (2000). Creating a caring community, *School Talk, 5*(4), 3.

Blau, S. (2003). *The literature workshop: Teaching texts and their readers.* Portsmouth, NH: Boynton/Cook.

Booth, D. (2006). *Reading doesn't matter anymore: Shattering the myths of literacy.* Ontario, Canada: Pembroke.

Calkins, L. (2000). *The art of teaching reading.* Boston: Allyn & Bacon.

Calkins, L. (2006). *A guide to the writing workshop.* Portsmouth, NH: Heinemann.

Clark, R. (2003). *The essential 55: An award-winning educator's rules for discovering the successful student in every child.* Santa Clara, CA: Hyperion.

Daniels, H., & Bizar, M. (2004). *Teaching the best practice way: Methods that matter, K–12.* Portland, ME: Stenhouse.

Daniels, H., & Zemelman, S. (2004). *Subjects matter: Every teacher's guide to content-area reading.* Portsmouth, NH: Heinemann.

Duthie, C. 1996. *True stories: Nonfiction literacy in the primary classroom.* Portland, ME: Stenhouse.

Five, C. L., & Egawa, K. (1998). What is it, and what does it look like, *School Talk, 3*(4), 1.

Fountas, I., & Pinnell, G. S. (1996). *Guided reading: Good first teaching for all children.* Portsmouth, NH: Heinemann.

Fried, R. (2002). *The passionate learner: How teachers and parents can help children reclaim the joy of discovery.* Boston, MA: Beacon Press.

Fried, R. (2005). *The game of school: Why we all play it, how it hurts kids, and what it will take to change it.* Hoboken, NJ: Jossey-Bass.

Gallagher, K. (2004). *Deeper reading: Comprehending challenging texts, 4–12.* Portland, ME: Stenhouse.

Goodman, Y. (1978). Kidwatching: An alternative to testing. *National Elementary Principal, 57*(4), 41–45.

Gregory, P. (2004). *The other Boleyn girl.* New York: Touchstone.

Hahn, M. (2002). *Reconsidering read-aloud.* Portland, ME: Stenhouse.

Hansen, J. 2004. *Tell me a story: Developmentally appropriate retelling strategies.* Newark, DE: International Reading Association.

Harvey, S., & Goudvis, A. (2000). *Strategies that work: Teaching comprehension to enhance understanding.* Portland, ME: Stenhouse.

Harwayne, S. 1999. *Going public: Priorities and practice at the Manhattan New School.* Portsmouth, NH: Heinemann.

Harwayne, S. 2000. *Lifetime guarantees: Toward ambitious literacy teaching.* Portsmouth, NH: Heinemann.

Hemingway, E. (1987). *A farewell to arms.* New York: Scribner.

Hindley, J. (1996). *In the company of children.* Portland, ME: Stenhouse.

Jago, C. (2004). *Classics in the classroom: Designing accessible literature lessons.* Portland, ME: Stenhouse.

Jago, C. (2005). Readers just want to have fun. *Voices in the Middle, 12*(3) 54.

Johnson, P. (2006). *One child at a time: Making the most of your time with struggling readers, K–6.* Portland, ME: Stenhouse.

Johnston, P. H. (2004). *Choice words: How our language affects children's learning.* Portland, ME: Stenhouse.

Mere, C. (2005). *More than guided reading: Finding the right instructional mix, K–3.* Portland, ME: Stenhouse.

Mermelstein, L. (2007). *Don't forget to share: The crucial last step in the writing workshop.* Portsmouth, NH: Heinemann.

Mills, H. (2007). Formative assessment: Helping students grow. *The Council Chronicle.*

O'Keefe, T. (1997). The habit of kidwatching. *School Talk.* 3(4) 4.

Ostrow, J. (1995). *A room with a different view.* Portland, ME: Stenhouse Publishers.

Quindlen, A. (1998) *How reading changed my life.* New York: Ballantine Books.

Routman, R. (2002). *Reading essentials:*

The specifics you need to teach reading well. Portsmouth, NH: Heinemann.

Santman, D. (2005). *Shades of meaning: Comprehension and interpretation in middle school.* Portsmouth, NH: Heinemann.

Sibberson, F., & Szymusiak, K. (2003). *Still learning to read: Teaching students in grades 3–6.* Portland, ME: Stenhouse.

Stepp, L. (2000). *Our last best shot: Guiding our children through early adolescence.* New York: Riverhead Trade.

Szymusiak, K., & Sibberson, F. (2001). *Beyond leveled books: Supporting transitional readers in grades 2–5.* Portland, ME: Stenhouse.

Taberski, S. (1995). *A close-up look at teaching reading: Focusing on children and our goals.* Portsmouth, NH: Heinemann.

Tovani, C. (2000). *I read it but I don't get it: Comprehension strategies for adolescent readers.* Portland, ME: Stenhouse.

Children's Publications Cited

Series

A–Z Mysteries

Amber Brown

Babymouse

Bailey School Kids

Boxcar Children

Captain Underpants

Children of the Lamp

Clementine

Horrible Harry

Ivy and Bean

Judy Moody

Junie B. Jones

Katie Kazoo, Switcheroo

Lemony Snicket's Series of Unfortunate Events

Magic Treehouse

Molly Moon

Magazines

Time for Kids

The Horn Book

Books

Aston, D. H. (2006). *An egg is quiet*. San Francisco: Chronicle Books.

Aston, D. H. (2007). *A seed is sleepy*. San Francisco: Chronicle Books.

Auch, M. J. (2005). *Wing nut*. New York: Henry Holt.

Avi. (1995). *Poppy*. New York: Simon & Schuster.

Avi. (2005). *The book without words: A fable of medieval magic*. Santa Clara, CA: Hyperion.

Barrows, A. (2007). *Ivy and Bean break the fossil record*. San Francisco: Chronicle Books.

Barry, D., & Pearson, R. (2006). *Peter and the shadow thieves*. New York: Disney Book Group.

Baylor, B. (1994). *The table where rich people sit*. New York: Atheneum.

Bondoux, A. (2005). *The destiny of Linus Hoppe*. New York: Delacorte Books for Young Readers.

Borden, L. (2005). *The journey that saved Curious George*. Boston: Houghton Mifflin.

Brisson, P. (1999). *The summer my father was ten*. Honesdale, PA: Boyds Mills Press.

Brown, M. W. (2005). *The runaway bunny*. Danvers, MA: HarperCollins.

Bunting, E. (2007). *Hurry! hurry!* Orlando, FL: Harcourt Children's Books.

Choldenko, G. (2004). *Al Capone does my shirts*. Toronto, Ontario, Canada: Putnam.

Clement, R. (1999). *Grandpa's teeth*. New York: HarperTrophy.

Clements, A (1996). *Frindle*. New York: Simon & Schuster.

Clements, A. (2002). *Things not seen*. New York: Puffin.

Clements, A. (2004). *The report card*. New York: Simon & Schuster.

Cline-Ransome, L. (2003). *Satchel Paige*. New York: Aladdin.

Cook, S., & Charlton, J. (2007). *Hey batta batta swing! The wild old days of baseball*. New York: Margaret K. McElderry.

Corey. S. (2000). *You forgot your skirt, Amelia Bloomer*. New York: Scholastic Press.

Creech, S. (2007). *Replay*. New York: HarperTrophy.

Danziger, P. (1994). *Amber Brown*. New York: Putnam Juvenile.

DiCamillo, K. (2000). *Because of Winn-Dixie*. Cambridge, MA: Candlewick Press.

DiCamillo, K. (2001). *The tiger rising*. Cambridge, MA: Candlewick Press.

DiCamillo, K. (2006). *The miraculous journey of Edward Tulane.* Cambridge, MA: Candlewick Press.

DiCamillo, K. (2006). *The tale of Despereaux: Being the story of a mouse, a princess, some soup and a spool of thread.* Cambridge, MA: Candlewick Press.

DuPrau, J. (2005). *The city of Ember.* New York: Yearling.

Eager, E. (1999). *Knight's castle.* Orlando, FL: Odyssey Classics.

Feiffer, J. (1999). *Bark, George.* New York: Laura Geringer Books.

Fletcher, R. (1998). *Flying solo.* Boston: Clarion Books.

Fletcher, R. (2005). *Marshfield dreams: When I was a kid.* New York: Henry Holt.

Fox, M. (1998). *Tough Boris.* Danvers, MA: Voyager Books.

Frazee, M. (2006). *Walk on: A guide for babies of all ages.* Orlando, FL: Harcourt Children's Books.

Frost, H. (2004). *Spinning through the universe.* New York: Farrar, Straus & Giroux.

Funke, C. (2003). *Inkheart.* New York: Scholastic Press.

Funke, C. (2005). *Dragon rider.* New York: Scholastic Press.

Gaiman, N. (2006). *Coraline.* New York: Harper Perennial.

Gibbons, G. (2000). *Pigs.* New York: Holiday House.

Gutman, D. (2007). *The homework machine.* New York: Aladdin.

Haddix, M. P. (2003). *Takeoffs and landings.* New York: Aladdin.

Hale, S. (2006). *Princess academy.* New York: Scholastic Press.

Hall, K. M. (2004). *Albino animals.* Plain City, OH: Darby Creek.

Henkes, K. (1999). *The Birthday room,* New York: Greenwillow Books.

Henkes, K. (2003). *Olive's ocean.* New York: Greenwillow Books.

Hiaasen, C. (2006). *Hoot.* New York: Yearling.

Jackson, D. M. (2003). *Hero dogs: Courageous canines in action.* New York: Little, Brown Books for Young Readers.

Jacques, B. (1987). *Redwall.* New York: Philomel.

Jeffers, O. (2006). *Lost and found.* Danvers, MA: HarperCollins.

Jenkins, E. (2006). *Toys go out: Being the adventures of a knowledgeable stingray, a toughy little buffalo, and someone called plastic.* New York: Schwartz & Wade.

Jenkins, S. (2007). *Dogs and cats.* Boston: Houghton Mifflin.

Kadohata, C. (2004). *Kira-Kira.* New York: Atheneum.

Kelly, I. (2007). *It's a butterfly's life.* New York: Holiday House.

Kerr, P. B. (2005). *Children of the lamp: The akhenaten adventure.* New York: Scholastic Press.

King-Smith, D. (1999). *A mouse called Wolf.* New York: Yearling.

Klise, K. (2001). *Trial by journal*. Danvers, MA: HarperCollins.

Konigsburg, E. L. (1972). *From the mixed-up files of Mrs. Basil E. Frankweiler*. New York: Atheneum.

Konigsburg, E. L. (1996). *The view from Saturday*. New York: Atheneum.

Konigsburg, E. L. (2004). *The outcasts of 19 Schuyler Place*. New York: Atheneum.

Konnecke, O. (2006). *Anthony and the girls*. New York: Farrar, Straus & Giroux.

L'Engle, M. (1962). *A wrinkle in time*. New York: Farrar, Straus & Giroux.

Levine, K. (2003). *Hana's suitcase*. Morton Grove, IL: Albert Whitman & Company.

Lewis, C. S. (1950). *The lion, the witch and the wardrobe*. Danvers, MA: HarperCollins.

Lin, G. (2007). *The year of the dog*. New York: Little, Brown Books for Young Readers.

Lipsyte, R. (2006). *Heroes of baseball: The men who made it America's favorite game*. New York: Atheneum.

Lord, C. (2006). *Rules*. New York: Scholastic Press.

Lovell, P. (2006). *Stand tall, Molly Lou Melton*. Toronto, Ontario, Canada: Putnam Juvenile.

Lowry, L. (2006). *Gossamer*. Boston: Houghton Mifflin.

MacLachlan, P. (1991). *Journey*. New York: Delacorte Press.

MacLachlan, P. (1993). *Baby*. New York: Delacorte Press.

Martin, A. M. (2000). *The doll people*. Santa Clara, CA: Hyperion.

Martin, A. M., & Danziger, P. (2000). *Snail mail no more*. New York: Scholastic Press.

Matthews, T. (2007). *Out of the egg*. Boston: Houghton Mifflin.

McDonald, M. (2003). *Judy Moody gets famous*. Cambridge, MA: Candlewick.

McDonald, M. (2006). *Stink: The incredible shrinking kid*. Cambridge, MA: Candlewick.

Merrill, J. (1974). *The toothpaste millionaire*. Boston: Houghton Mifflin.

Meschenmoser, S. (2006). *Learning to fly*. La Jolla, CA: Kane/Miller.

Mikaelsen, B. (2001). *Touching spirit bear*. New York: HarperCollins.

Newman, J. (2006). *Hippo! No, rhino*. New York: Little, Brown Books for Young Readers.

O'Connor, B. (2007). *How to steal a dog*. New York: Farrar, Straus & Giroux.

Park, B. (1982). *Skinnybones*. Boston: Clarion.

Park, F., & Park, G. (2000). *The royal bee*. Honesdale, PA: Boyds Mills Press.

Park, L. S. (2001). *A single shard*. Boston: Clarion.

Park, L. S. (2005). *Project Mulberry*. New York: Yearling.

Pennypacker, S. (2006). *Clementine*. Santa Clara, CA: Hyperion.

Reynolds, P. (2006). *So few of me*. Cambridge, MA: Candlewick.

Robbins, K. (2006). *Pumpkins*. New York: Roaring Brook Press.

Rosen, M. J. (2006). *Balls!* Plain City, OH: Darby Creek.

Rylant, C. (1995). *The Van Gogh Café*. San Diego, CA: Harcourt Brace.

Rylant, C. (2005). *Boris*. Orlando, FL: Harcourt.

Rylant, C, (1985). *Every living thing*. New York: Atheneum/Richard Jackson Books.

Sachar, L. (1998). *Holes*. New York: Farrar, Straus & Giroux.

Scieszka, J. (2005). *Guys write for guys read*. New York: Viking Juvenile.

Selznick, B. (2007). *The invention of Hugo Cabret*. New York: Scholastic Press.

Singer, M. (2006). *What stinks?* Plain City, OH: Darby Creek.

Slavin, B. (2005). *Transformed: How everyday things are made*. Toronto, ON Ontario, Canada: Kids Can Press.

Snicket, L. (1999). *The bad beginning*. Danvers, MA: HarperCollins.

Spinelli, J. (1996). *Crash*. New York: Knopf Books for Young Readers.

Spinelli, J. (1998). *Knots in my yo-yo string*. New York: Knopf for Young Readers.

Spinelli, J. (2003). *Loser*. Danvers, MA: HarperTrophy.

Stewart, D. (2005). *You wouldn't want to explore with Sir Frances Drake! A pirate you'd rather not know*. London, England: Franklin Watts.

Tesar, J., Glassman, B. S., & Italiano, B. (1999). *Kidbits*. Farmington Hills, MI: Blackbirch Press.

Thimmesh, C. (2002). *Girls think of everything: Stories of ingenious inventions by women*. Boston: Houghton Mifflin.

Turner, P. S. (2005). *Gorilla doctors: Saving endangered great apes*. Boston: Houghton Mifflin.

Van Draanen, W. (2004). *Shredderman: Secret identity*. New York: Scholastic Press.

Watt, M. (2006). *Scaredy squirrel*. Toronto, Ontario, Canada: Kids Can Press.

Weeks, S. (2004). *So B. It*. Danvers, MA: HarperTrophy.

Weiss, E. (2000). *Odd jobs: The wackiest jobs you've never heard of*. New York: Aladdin.

Williams, V. (2001). *Amber was brave, Essie was smart*. New York: Greenwillow Books.

Woodson, J. (2001). *The other side*. Toronto, Ontario, Canada: Putnam Juvenile.

Wulffson, D. (1999). *The kid who invented the popsicle: And other surprising stories about inventions*. New York: Puffin.

Wulffson, D. (2001). *The kid who invented the trampoline: More surprising stories about inventions*. New York: Dutton Juvenile.

Yin, (2006). *Brothers*. New York: Philomel.
Yoo, T. (2007). *The little red fish*. New York: Dial.

Index

Gutman, Dan, 89, 161
Guys Write for Guys Read (Scieszka), 41

H

Haddix, Margaret Peterson, 139
Hahn, Mary Lee, 80
Hale, Shannon, 148-149
Hansen, Jill, 133
Harvey, Stephanie, 107
Harwayne, Shelley, 146, 159
Hiaasen, Carl, 105
Hindley, Joanne, 23, 118
Hippo! No, Rhino (Newman), 41
Historical fiction, 111
Holes (Sachar), 83, 89
Holm, Jennifer, 65
Holm, Matt, 65
Home reading logs
    conversations around, 74–75
    reflection sheet based on, 187
The Homework Machine (Gutman), 89
Hoot (Hiaasen), 105
How Reading Changed My Life (Quindlen), 46
How to Steal a Dog (O'Connor), 82, 152

I

I Read It, but I Don't Get It (Tovani), 12
In the Company of Children (Hindley), 23, 118
In the Middle (Atwell), 15, 53, 155
Independent reading
    assessment during, 67–79, 167
    assessment of, 166
    messages sent during, 27
    new books in, 66
    observation during, 28–29
    reading logs in, 29–31, 67–73
    setting the stage for, 27–28
    student self-discovery in, 62
    texts for, 63-66
Individual reading conferences, 49
    assessment of, 166
    on comprehension, 148–149
    coupled with whole-class share time, 155–157
    on fluency, 149-151
    goals for, 147
    on keeping track of characters, 153
    learning from students in, 153–154
    literary chitchat in, 154–155
    messages sent during, 49
    on nonfiction, 153
    questions asked in, 148
    on text features, 149
    on theme, 152-153
    on vocabulary, 152
Information gathering, about students, 19, 25
Inkheart (Funke), 85, 155
Intermediate texts, characteristics of, 11
Interviews, in reading workshop, 20, 54–56, 160, 182–183
The Invention of Hugo Cabret (Selznick), 89, 152
It's a Butterfly's Life (Kelly), 114
Ivy and Bean series (Barrows), 65, 118

J

Jacques, Brian, 154
Jago, Carol, 12, 98, 180
Jenkins, Steve, 63
Johnson, Pat, 26, 108
Johnston, Peter, 11, 107
Journey (MacLachlan), 82, 83, 85, 99
Judy Moody Gets Famous (McDonald), 85
Just-right books, 116–117

K

Kadohata, Cynthia, 83, 133, 153–154, 155
Kelly, Irene, 114
Kerr, P. B., 155
The Kid Who Invented the Popsicle (Wulffson), 113
The Kid Who Invented the Trampoline (Wulffson), 162
Kidbits (Tesar et al.), 153
Kira-Kira (Kadohata), 83, 133, 153–154, 155
Klise, Kate, 89, 149
Knots in My Yo-Yo String (Spinelli), 41
Konigsburg, E. L., 82, 86, 88, 90, 154

L

Learning, ownership of, 17
Lewis, C. S., 82, 141
Library, classroom, 64–65
Lifetime Guarantees (Harwayne), 146
The Lion, the Witch, and the Wardrobe (Lewis), 82, 141
Literary elements, 98-99
    reflection sheet for, 199
The Literature Workshop (Blau), 12
The Little Red Fish (Yoo), 161
Lord, Cynthia, 93, 99, 100
Loser (Spinelli), 133

M

MacLachlan, Patricia, 82, 83, 85
Marshfield Dreams (Fletcher), 41, 82
Martin, Ann M., 152, 154
McDonald, Megan, 85
Mere, Cathy, 122
Mermelstein, Leah, 157
Metaphors, 11
Mikaelsen, Ben, 82, 90, 140
Mills, Heidi, 77
Mini-lessons
    advantages of, 39
    books to support, 41
    characteristics of, 107–108
    early, 39–40
    examples of early, 41–46
    linked to reading workshop, 109–110
    nonfiction, 112–114
    readers' lives woven into, 110–111
    state standards and, 108–109
    structure of, 108
    student-led, 118–119
    teacher experience woven into, 110
    topics for, 108–111
The Miraculous Journey of Edward Tulane (DiCamillo), 93–97
Molly Moon series (Byng), 155
More Than Guided Reading (Mere), 122

N

Newman, Jeff, 41
Nonfiction
    conferences on, 153
    in independent reading, 63, 64–65
    as literature, 111
    mini-lessons on, 112–114
    narrative, 112–113
    popular works of, 162
    previewing, 113–114
    purpose for reading, 114
    teacher attitudes toward, 112
Notebooks, read-aloud, 37–39
    assessment of, 168–171
    impact on student learning, 90–92
    improvement of, 168–171
    organization of, 95–97
    reflection sheets for, 189–190

understanding fostered by, 93–97
unsuccessful use of, 92–93
using, 87–88, 160

O

Observation, 38, 160
    and assessment, 19
    during independent reading, 28–29, 77
    during mini-lessons, 42, 109–110
    of small groups, 44
O'Connor, Barbara, 82, 152
Odd Jobs (Weiss), 43–44
One Child at a Time (Johnson), 26, 108
Opinions, supporting, 43–46
Ostrow, Jill, 10
The Other Boleyn Girl (Gregory), 111
Our Last Best Shot (Stepp), 12
The Outcasts of 19 Schuyler Place (Konigsburg), 82, 154

P

Parent conferences, 57
    assessment web for, 60
Park, Linda Sue, 154
The Passionate Learner (Fried), 7, 13
Pearson, Ridley, 119
Pennypacker, Sara, 118
Peter and the Shadow Thieves (Barry & Pearson), 119
Pigs (Gibbons), 113
Pinnell, Gay Su, 121
Poetry, in independent reading, 63, 65
Poppy (Avi), 85
Predictions, making, 115
Previewing, book, 35–36, 84–85
    nonfiction, 113–114
    questions raised during, 93–95
Primary texts, characteristics of, 11
Princess Academy (Hale), 148-149
Problem solving with students, 104
Progress reports, 172–173
Project Mulberry (Park), 154
Purpose, for nonfiction reading, 114

Q

Quindlen, Anna, 46
Quotes, books with, 90

R

Read-alouds, 32, 34–35
    assessment during, 34, 81, 167
    assessment of, 166
    and big questions, 99–100
    literature for, 33, 81–83
    learning from, 114–116
    messages sent during, 32
    notebooks and sticky notes for, 37–39, 87–97, 160, 168–171
    previewing for, 35–36, 84–85
    short novels for, 83
    solving problems with, 103–105
    teaching value of, 34, 80–81
    for thinking skills, 83–87
    using individual copies of books for, 89
    written response to, 101–103
Readers
    assessment of. See Assessment
    community of, 12–13
    importance of knowing, 10–11, 25
    obstacles for, 11–12
    reluctant, 77–78
    self-knowledge of, 46
    student goals for, 12–13